LOVE UNKNOWN

Also by John Barton and published by SPCK:

People of the Book?
(1988)

John Barton

LOVE UNKNOWN

Meditations on the Death and Resurrection of Jesus

First published in Great Britain in 1990 by
SPCK
Holy Trinity Church
Marylebone Road
London NW1 4DU

Second impression 1990

The Scripture quotations in this publication are from the Revised Standard
Version of the Bible, copyrighted 1946, 1952, © 1971, 1973 by the Division of
Christian Education of the National Council of the Churches of Christ in the
USA, and are used by permission.

We are grateful to the following for permission to reproduce copyright material:

Bristol Classical Press for the extract from 'The Problem of Pain' by David
Brown in Robert Morgan (ed.) *The Religion of the Incarnation: Anglican Essays
in Commemoration of Lux Mundi*.

Constable Publishers for the extract from *Peter Abelard* by Helen Waddell.

Constable Publishers and Mary M. Martin for the extracts from *Medieval Latin
Lyrics* by Helen Waddell.

The Movement for the Ordination of Women and Women in Theology, Napier
Hall, Hide Place, London SW1P 4NT, for the extracts from *All Desires Known*
by Janet Morley.

The Stanbrook Abbey Trustees for the extracts from *More Latin Lyrics from
Virgil to Milton* by Helen Waddell.

British Library Cataloguing in Publication Data

Barton, John, *1948–*
    Love unknown: meditations on the death and resurrection of Jesus
    1. Christian doctrine. Eschatology
    I. Title
    236

ISBN 0-281-04440-6

Printed in Great Britain by
WBC Print Ltd, Bristol

For the people of The Church in Abingdon

Love Unknown

My song is love unknown,
My Saviour's love to me,
Love to the loveless shown,
That they might lovely be.
O, who am I,
That for my sake
My Lord should take
Frail flesh, and die?

He came from his blest throne,
Salvation to bestow:
But men made strange, and none
The longed-for Christ would know.
But O, my Friend,
My Friend indeed,
Who at my need
His life did spend!

Sometimes they strew his way,
And his sweet praises sing;
Resounding all the day
Hosannas to their King.
Then 'Crucify!'
Is all their breath,
And for his death
They thirst and cry.

Why, what hath my Lord done?
　　What makes this rage and spite?
He made the lame to run,
　　He gave the blind their sight.
　　　　Sweet injuries!
　　　　　　Yet they at these
　　　　　　Themselves displease,
　　　　And 'gainst him rise.

They rise, and needs will have
　　My dear Lord made away;
A murderer they save,
　　The Prince of Life they slay.
　　　　Yet cheerful he
　　　　　　To suffering goes,
　　　　　　That he his foes
　　　　From thence might free.

In life, no house, no home
　　My Lord on earth might have;
In death, no friendly tomb
　　But what a stranger gave.
　　　　What may I say?
　　　　　　Heav'n was his home;
　　　　　　But mine the tomb
　　　　Wherein he lay.

Here might I stay and sing.
　　No story so divine;
Never was love, dear King,
　　Never was grief like thine!
　　　　This is my Friend,
　　　　　　In whose sweet praise
　　　　　　I all my days
　　　　Could gladly spend.

SAMUEL CROSSMAN (1624–83)

Contents

Foreword

Human life is unpredictable – full of sorrows no one can foresee and of joys that come unlooked for. But Christians often see the life, death, and resurrection of Jesus as an exception to this rule. The 'drama' of Easter seems to unfold like a great play whose author is God, and in which each actor plays a predestined role. The starting point for this book is the conviction that cross and resurrection alike are travestied when they are seen in this way. In entering into our world and sharing in its suffering, God in Christ accepts the uncertainty and unpredictability that are part of the human lot. In embodying God's love, Jesus was subject to the randomness and uncertainty that we experience as the ultimate threat to human life; and his resurrection is a sign of unexpected hope beyond final despair.

In Holy Week this year I was invited to preach each day in the parish church of St Mary and All Saints, Chesterfield – famous throughout Britain as 'the church with the crooked spire' – and the core of this book consists of the addresses I gave. I took as my 'text' the poem 'My song is love unknown', which has been popular as a hymn in many Christian churches since it was set by John Ireland to the melody called 'Love Unknown'. It is a pleasure to thank Brian Cooper, the vicar, who invited me to participate in his church's worship, and also Ann and John Duncan and all the other people whose hospitality made it such a stimulating week. Other chapters have been used in the three churches in Abingdon where I regularly preach: St Helen, St Michael and All Angels, and St Nicolas. I have lived in Abingdon now for twelve years, and one of the many pleasures of life there has been the closeness and warmth of relations among Christians of different communions in the town. Last year this found expression in a local ecumenical agreement in which all the main denominations agreed henceforth to be known corporately as, simply, 'The Church in Abingdon'. So it is under that name that I should like to dedicate this book to all my fellow Christians in the town and to thank them for their friendship and support.

Readers will use the book in whatever way they find useful. But bearing in mind that some will wish to be helped by it in prayer or

Bible study I have begun each chapter with a passage from Scripture, and concluded with a prayer. The biblical quotations here and throughout the book are from the Revised Standard Version. With a few exceptions the prayers are taken from the remarkable collection by Janet Morley, *All Desires Known*[1] – prayers whose insight and resonance have taught me a great deal.

The themes that the book handles are ones on which I suppose no Christian preacher would even aspire to be 'original'; but even so I am aware of how very derivative my ideas are. My own professional field is the study of the Old Testament, and my knowledge of technical works about the passion and resurrection stories in the Gospels, about theories of the atonement, and about the philosophy of religion is at a very amateur level. But this book is not meant for professional theologians, though I can only hope not to have said too many naive or ignorant things that will provoke any colleagues who may read it. I have every confidence that they will tell me if I have! Friends, teachers, students and chance acquaintances have all influenced my thinking just as much as books; and the discerning reader will rightly suspect that personal experience (my own and that of people dear to me) lies behind some of the chapters, though the book as a whole is in no sense an exercise in spiritual autobiography. My wife Mary in particular will know how much it owes to shared reflection on the themes of suffering and resurrection.

There are three theologians, however, whose influence I should like to acknowledge explicitly. John Austin Baker, now Bishop of Salisbury, was one of my tutors when I was an undergraduate; and his great book *The Foolishness of God*[2] was published while he was subsequently supervising my doctoral research on the Old Testament. The seeds it sowed in my mind have germinated slowly ever since, and much of what is said here is owed to his inspiration. His book ends with the same poem that I have taken as my guiding thread.

Gerhard Sauter, Professor of Systematic Theology in Bonn, has been a good friend to me over the twelve years that the Theology faculties in Bonn and Oxford have enjoyed a close co-operative relationship, and I am conscious of a huge debt to his ideas – I only hope that I have not distorted or trivialized them. In any case I am of course entirely responsible for whatever I have done with thoughts borrowed from others.

My third debt is to someone I never knew. Helen Waddell –

translator, poet, medievalist, and novelist – will presumably not appear in any account of theology in the twentieth century; but since I discovered her books in my teens they have meant more to me than most 'professional' theology. There are writers who set the standards to which you aspire even while knowing you will not reach them; but there are others on reading whom you know at once that you are in the presence of absolute genius, and that simple gratitude is all that is either possible or necessary. Today is the hundredth anniversary of Helen Waddell's birth, and it is as a very tiny acknowledgement of what I owe to her 'Abelardian' theology of the cross that I have included a number of quotations from her translations in what seemed appropriate places; as well as the famous passage which I think of (as though it were a Gospel parable) simply as 'The Rabbit', from her novel *Peter Abelard* – often enough quoted in books like this but still, surely, inexhaustible.

John Barton
St Cross College, Oxford
31 May 1989

CHAPTER ONE

The Necessary Path

> We see Jesus, who for a little while was made lower than the angels, crowned with glory and honour because of the suffering of death, so that by the grace of God he might taste death for every one. For it was fitting that he, for whom and by whom all things exist, in bringing many sons to glory, should make the pioneer of their salvation perfect through suffering. For he who sanctifies and those who are sanctified have all one origin. That is why he is not ashamed to call them brethren, saying, 'I will proclaim thy name to my brethren, in the midst of the congregation I will praise thee.'
>
> Hebrews 2.9–12

At the end of St Luke's Gospel, the risen Christ appears to the disciples on the road to Emmaus, and reproaches them for having failed to understand the necessity of the suffering he has endured. ' "O foolish men, and slow of heart to believe all that the prophets have spoken! Was it not necessary that the Christ should suffer these things and enter into his glory?" And beginning with Moses and all the prophets, he interpreted to them in all the scriptures the things concerning himself' (Luke 24.25–7). Commentators down the ages have pored over the Old Testament ('Moses and the prophets') to discover the verses where the sufferings of God's Messiah are foretold. For the picture St Luke's account conjures up for us is of Jesus as a man of destiny: one who believed that the details of his life, both small and great, were written in the Scriptures, and who set himself to fulfil the vocation he found set down there, which had necessarily to lead through suffering and death. The Passion Narratives in the Gospels convey a sense that a great drama, prearranged by God, is being worked out; even the traitor was foreordained to his role. And so the necessity that the Messiah should suffer seems part of a great design, whose lines can be discerned by those who read the Old Testament Scriptures with care. Thus the sufferings of Jesus, Christians have often believed, were necessary in the strict sense, for God had planned them from all eternity. Without suffering the divine purpose for the world could not be accomplished, for 'without the shedding of blood there is no forgiveness of sins' (Heb. 9.22).

And so we might look through the Old Testament for the proof texts that would show how Christ had to suffer; but we should look in vain. There is Isaiah 53, read in many churches on Good Friday, about the suffering servant of the Lord:

> He was despised and rejected by men;
>> a man of sorrows, and acquainted with grief;
> and as one from whom men hide their faces
>> he was despised, and we esteemed him not.
> Surely he has borne our griefs
>> and carried our sorrows;
> yet we esteemed him stricken,
>> smitten by God, and afflicted.
> But he was wounded for our transgressions,
>> he was bruised for our iniquities;
> upon him was the chastisement that made us whole,
>> and with his stripes we are healed . . .
>
> He was oppressed, and he was afflicted,
>> yet he opened not his mouth;
> like a lamb that is led to the slaughter,
>> and like a sheep that before its shearers is dumb,
>> so he opened not his mouth (Isa. 53.3–7).

There is an uncanny likeness between this prophecy and what Jesus suffered, even though only in rather general terms. But there is scarcely anything else. In telling the story of the death of Jesus the New Testament writers tracked down all the possible allusions they could find in the Scriptures, and at times they may even have adjusted the story they were telling to make it fit the texts they had found more closely; but even so they could not show that everything had been foretold in the Scriptures. No one reading the Old Testament could possibly work out that God's Messiah would endure the sufferings that Jesus endured. Only a massive dose of hindsight produced the proof texts that Christians have used to show the necessity of Christ's sufferings.

But perhaps this does not matter. For perhaps what Jesus gave his disciples after the resurrection was not so much a list of proof texts, as an insight into the kind of God to whom the Old Testament bears witness, and the kind of person such a God would choose as his servant and messenger and son. 'It was necessary for the Christ to suffer'; but not because it had been laid down in a heavenly book or an earthly scripture, not because God desires suffering or insists on exacting it from a victim before he will forgive human beings their sins. It was necessary for the Christ to suffer because the character of the God who was known in Israel, and whose agent Jesus was on earth, is such that the way of the cross was in practice bound to be the way he would follow. Jesus did not come preaching the good news of the kingdom of God *in order* to get himself executed, as though he were stage-managing his own execution – a peculiarly sick idea, though one that many Christians seem willing to accept. He came to embody the love of God for his creation, accepting the consequences of doing so whatever these might be.

As we reflect on the suffering and death of Jesus we do not gaze with bewilderment at an inscrutable divine plan, trembling with horror at a God who sends an innocent man to death because he desires blood, or for some other reason that human beings can never know. The passion and death of the Lord are not a pagan sacrifice, nor are they the playing out in flesh of a terrible tragedy scripted by God. The death of Jesus is not the cruel fate of one who was the victim of the gods. Nor do we read about the passion to strengthen our resolve to suffer with Jesus, despite the hymn which says:

> In thy most bitter passion
> My heart to share doth cry,
> With thee for my salvation
> Upon the Cross to die.[1]

The feeling is understandable, but it is not the reason for meditating on the cross. Jesus did not suffer and die so that we should suffer and die, too, even if only in imagination. Christians commemorate the sufferings of their Lord with a song, and this is what they sing:

> My song is love unknown,
> My Saviour's love to me,
> Love to the loveless shown,
> That they might lovely be.
> O, who am I,

3

> That for my sake
> My Lord should take
> Frail flesh, and die?

Jesus did not come to placate an angry God, to do the bidding of an inscrutable God, or to be a model for submission to a cruel God. He came to be the love of God; to show in our own 'frail flesh' not what God demands but what God is prepared to give. He came to call God's own people back to himself, and through them to extend the divine call to all mankind. And he was prepared, as God is prepared, to do it by teaching and example, by successful healings and signs and wonders, but also if necessary by suffering and death. As things turned out, it was indeed necessary. Like St Paul after him, Jesus remained true to his mission 'in honour and dishonour, in ill repute and good repute . . . as unknown, and yet well known; as sorrowful, yet always rejoicing; as poor, yet making many rich; as having nothing, and yet possessing everything' (2 Cor. 6.8–10).

The life and death of Jesus are to be seen as a sign or icon of the character of God himself. God, so the writers of the Old Testament believed, is involved with his people; their joys are his joys, their sufferings are his sufferings. But in the Old Testament that is said more in hope than in certainty. By an act of faith prophets can say such things as 'in all their afflictions he [God] was afflicted' (Isa. 63.9) or 'I took them up in my arms . . . I led them with cords of compassion, with the bands of love . . . I bent down to them and fed them' (Hos. 11.3–4); but how in the end can the infinite and inexhaustible being who is God suffer and have compassion? Christians say that Jesus is the sign that indeed he can, and does. The credibility of a God who says he is involved in human life can be tested only in a rather literal way, and Jesus is the point at which it was tested; and the result was positive. Jesus 'had to' suffer because divine love identifies itself with the human condition, and that is a bitter-sweet combination of pleasure and pain; in William Blake's words,

> Man was made for Joy and Woe;
> And when this we rightly know,
> Thro' the World we safely go.[2]

To take human beings seriously is to accept this mixture of joy and woe, which is our tragedy and yet also our dignity. The mystery on which Christians reflect with thanksgiving is that God himself knows the human lot from the inside. He, like us, knows what it is to hang suspended between these two poles, and to experience joy not as infinite serenity but as a fierce happiness snatched from the jaws of darkness and despair.

> For Mercy has a human heart,
>   Pity a human face;
> And Love, the human form divine,
>   And Peace, the human dress.[3]

To 'have a human face' – to share the human condition – means that God has to put himself in a situation where the outcome of his actions is uncertain, just as it is for us. The passion and death of Jesus are not something God had neatly mapped out. Jesus' life and death alike contained the unexpected, joys that could not be foreseen and sorrows that he could not be forearmed against. In this book we shall reflect on the way God brought hope and joy to the human race by showing us, in Jesus, that he is willing to be subject to the same forces that so baffle and bewilder us, and in that way to respond to the human tragedy in a human way. Jesus is the human face of God – or, better, Jesus is the demonstration that God has a human face. Through him we do not bow down before naked power or stand in bewilderment before incomprehensible glory, but enter into a heart of love. And this is why the Christ had to suffer; because in him God, as the Letter to the Hebrews puts it, was not ashamed to call us his brothers and sisters, and that could be so only if he was prepared to share in the light and shade which is the stuff of all human life.

> Jesus our brother,
> you followed the necessary path
> and were broken on our behalf.
> May we neither cling to our pain
> where it is futile,
> nor refuse to embrace the cost
> when it is required of us;
> that in losing our selves for your sake,
> we may be brought to new life.[4]

CHAPTER TWO *The Outsider*

Jesus said to them, 'Doubtless you will quote to me this proverb, "Physician, heal yourself; what we have heard you did at Capernaum, do here also in your own country."' And he said, 'Truly, I say to you, no prophet is acceptable in his own country. But in truth, I tell you, there were many widows in Israel in the days of Elijah, when the heaven was shut up three years and six months, when there came a great famine over all the land; and Elijah was sent to none of them but only to Zarephath, in the land of Sidon, to a woman who was a widow. And there were many lepers in Israel in the time of the prophet Elisha; and none of them was cleansed, but only Naaman the Syrian.' When they heard this, all in the synagogue were filled with wrath. And they rose up and put him out of the city, and led him to the brow of the hill on which their city was built, that they might throw him down headlong.

Luke 4.23–9

My grandmother had a simple scheme for classifying the rest of the human race which would be the envy of any sociologist. She divided her fellow men and women into two categories: 'family' and 'strangers'. 'Family' meant primarily blood relatives; although favoured in-laws did sometimes graduate to being at least practically 'family', in times of crisis the basic simple division tended to reassert itself. And friends remained 'strangers' however long they had been friends, and were welcome only on certain conditions.

The problems this scheme made for other people were substantial, but are not my point here. What is worth seeing is how fundamental a distinction like this has been in the minds of most of the human race at most times in history. Human society cannot survive without a distinction between 'us' and 'them'; and yet it cannot survive either if the distinction becomes so rigid that people react to outsiders with unrelieved aggression and hatred. This is the tragedy of being human: we must protect ourselves against the danger of being engulfed by strangers, and yet the protection can become self-defeating and self-destructive if it is not controlled. The ultimate example of this, of course, is seen in the perils of modern weapons systems, where we all know that there is a danger that over-efficient self-defence may itself be construed as aggression. Being over-prepared not to lose a war can actually embroil a nation in a war it cannot win. How this dilemma is to be resolved is another question – not to be answered in a book such as this.

Now seen from a sociological point of view religion is in general a mechanism for maintaining the identity of groups to which people belong and defending them against outsiders. People who belong to a religious tradition are in effect defining themselves as forming a larger family, but distinguishing themselves from the 'strangers' who make up the rest of the human race. A religious commitment becomes a kind of tribal allegiance, and religions often develop ways of policing the frontiers of the religious community to make sure that only the real insiders are inside, and that people cannot get in by stealth if they do not really believe in what the religion stands for, or practise what it teaches. Judaism and Christianity, as they have developed down the years, are no exception to this rule. Both are deeply concerned with identity, with authority, and with initiation rites that make it possible to decide without doubt who is in and who is out.

But at the beginning of both religions lies a startling breakthrough which (rightly understood) calls in question this social function of religion as a method of distinguishing 'family' from 'strangers'.[1] The prophets of Israel discovered, for the first time in human history, the truth that there is only one God and that all men and women are equally his creation and equally under his care and concern. Good and bad, rich and poor, black and white, religious and irreligious, all people are the children of the one God. What is more, they said, God's commitment to the truth that all are insiders – members of his family – is so intense that he intervenes to even out the unevennesses which the human need for self-preservation and the human drive to self-assertion inevitably introduce into the world. In other words, he actively takes the side of exactly those people who are regarded by others as strangers or outcasts or rejects. Hence the Old Testament's commitment to the cause of the widows and the orphans, its championing of the rights of resident aliens and slaves. This is only one theme in the Old Testament, alongside the equally characteristic distaste for all that is foreign and the concern with keeping the Jewish race pure; but it *is* one theme, and it is linked with belief in the one God of all.

> For the LORD your God is God of gods and Lord of lords, the great, the mighty, and the terrible God, who is not partial and takes no bribe. He executes justice for the fatherless and the widow, and loves the sojourner, giving him food and clothing. Love the sojourner [i.e. the resident alien] therefore; for you were sojourners in the land of Egypt (Deut. 10.17–19).

Christianity owes its origins to a moment when this insight was recaptured within the context of a Judaism that was in danger of losing sight of it. The time when Palestine was occupied by a foreign power was a strange time for a revival of the insight that God loves outsiders; but so it proved. Jesus of Nazareth seems to have attracted the critical attention of the Jewish leadership partly through his miracles and his message of impending divine judgement on the world. But, after all, those things were what one had come to expect from Galilean holy men. He became a thorn in the flesh much more because, like the prophets of old, he pronounced God's blessing on those who were socially unacceptable and outcast. It is very hard to identify just what it was in Jesus' teaching that was offensive *enough* to his contemporaries to get him executed by presenting a trumped-up charge of treason to the Roman authorities, but it almost certainly had something to do with this theme. He associated freely with collaborators and tax-collectors, and threatened the boundaries of properly religious Judaism by refusing to draw distinctions between 'us' and 'them'. If Jesus 'came to his own home, and his own people received him not' (John 1.11), it was above all because he refused to acknowledge that there were any creatures of God who were more his own people than others. This affected his relations with his family in the literal sense, as well as with the wider family of Jewish people in general. The Gospels are full of difficult sayings to the effect that Jesus' real 'brothers and sisters' are not his blood relatives, but those – many of them obvious sinners by any standards – who had associated themselves with him and his disciples. Jesus' life was a protest against the human defence mechanisms which keep outsiders at bay.

The disciples misunderstood this just as much as anyone else, seeing the new community which they formed as needing to define its own limits and keep itself safe. Remember the incident where the disciples complain that someone is casting out devils in Jesus' name when he isn't a proper member of their club; and Jesus' obviously agonized despair that they have understood so little what his life's work is all about (see Mark 9.38–41). What crucified Jesus, first metaphorically and then literally, was the human drive to form a club and keep out non-members. It is the most human and harmless of tendencies, without which human society is impossible. Yet it is also the most demonic and destructive of forces, repeated again and again in the human race's long tale of hatred and malice and genocide. Families show us the whole problem in a miniature form. We cannot live without them; yet they provide the natural habitat for all that is most destructive and vicious in human life. In family life there are opportunities for the greatest love one human being can feel or show for another, and at the same time for the ultimate selfishness of a self-defensive cocoon. And the problem – and here's the rub – is insoluble. We perish unless we band together in groups; but when we do, we destroy each other, either psychologically or physically. And more than anyone we destroy the person who points this out to us, because we cannot afford to be challenged on the matter; it threatens the defences which keep strangers and other hostile forces at bay.

The life and death of Jesus, so Christians believe, are God's way of handling the problems of the human condition. Not of solving them: the problems really are insoluble, and to ask why God does not solve them is to ask in effect why he did not make a different world altogether, or why he does not simply destroy this one. Jesus is not God's *answer* to the contradiction between the human need for security and safety and the inevitable fact that the quest for security and safety lead to aggression and ultimately to self-destruction for the human race. For there is no answer; the contradiction is endemic to being human. Jesus is God's own willingness to get involved in the contradiction and to experience it from the inside. He came to warn of the dangers of establishing an exclusive club, and to challenge people to reject the drive that makes them exclude others – and of course in the process to be excluded himself, and to take the consequences.

> He came from his blest throne,
>   Salvation to bestow:
> But men made strange, and none

The longed-for Christ would know.
But O, my Friend,
My Friend indeed,
Who at my need
His life did spend!

Perhaps a Galilean was the ideal choice for this task, for Galileans were already half-outsiders, from a Jewish point of view, regarded with the kind of suspicion my grandmother showed towards her in-laws; you couldn't tell whether they were 'family' or not. Galileans were Jews, one supposed; at least they had to be given the benefit of the doubt. But one didn't expect lectures from them on how God wanted the world organized, and a Galilean Messiah was scarcely a serious proposition. Yet it is the life of a Galilean in which generations have seen the character of God made manifest, and it was on the shores of the sea of Galilee that the silence of eternity was interpreted by love. Even God cannot do what cannot in the nature of the case be done, and therefore even God cannot resolve the contradiction, embedded deep in human nature, between the need to exclude and the need not to be excluded. But one thing God can do. He can allow himself to be torn apart by the contradiction and so give hope to those who in their own lives, great or small, are crucified on this particular cross, which is the cross that tortures all mankind.

Look on thy God, Christ hidden in our flesh.
A bitter word, the cross, and bitter sight:
Hard rind without, to hold the heart of heaven.
Yet sweet it is; for God upon that tree
Did offer up his life: upon that rood
My Life hung, that my life might stand in God.[2]

The life of the carpenter from Nazareth in Galilee is a symbol that God's way is to allow himself to be rejected by the people to whom he belongs most closely: to discover by practice what it is like to be an outsider who does not hate and envy the people inside, and an insider who does not want to keep anyone locked out. In a world where everyone must be at the same time an insider and an outsider, where there is no possibility that the tension can ever be resolved, where human beings are alternately longing for home and yearning for what is strange and new, in such a world the carpenter who wandered from Galilee to Jerusalem, to be at the centre of his people so that they could reject him and throw him out of their city, is a sign that God understands, and does not despise the strange creatures that human beings are.

> Christ leads me through no darker rooms
>   Than he went through before;
> He that into God's kingdom comes
>   Must enter by this door.[3]

———————

Holy God,
we are born into a world
tissued and structured by sin.
When we proclaim our innocence
and seek to accuse each other,
give us the grace to know that we are naked;
that we may cry out to you alone
through Jesus Christ.[4]

CHAPTER THREE

Time and Chance

'Therefore I tell you, do not be anxious about your life, what you shall eat or what you shall drink, nor about your body, what you shall put on. Is not life more than food, and the body more than clothing? Look at the birds of the air: they neither sow nor reap nor gather into barns, and yet your heavenly Father feeds them. Are you not of more value than they? And which of you by being anxious can add one cubit to his span of life? And why are you anxious about clothing? Consider the lilies of the field, how they grow; they neither toil nor spin; yet I tell you, even Solomon in all his glory was not arrayed like one of these. But if God so clothes the grass of the field, which today is alive and tomorrow is thrown into the oven, will he not much more clothe you, O men of little faith? Therefore do not be anxious, saying, "What shall we eat?" or "What shall we drink?" or "What shall we wear?" For the Gentiles seek all these things; and your heavenly Father knows that you need them all. But seek first his kingdom and his righteousness, and all these things shall be yours as well. Therefore do not be anxious about tomorrow, for tomorrow will be anxious for itself. Let the day's own trouble be sufficient for the day.'

Matthew 6.25–34

Near where I live there is a small church which has a notice-board on which to display a text or slogan for the edification of passers-by. The text changes with the seasons. Last Christmas it had the starkest one I've seen, which read simply:

JESUS WAS BORN TO DIE

No Christian, I suppose, could disagree with that; yet surely as a five-word summary of the gospel message it misses the heart of what Christians believe in. The underlying thought is perhaps that the one thing Jesus had to do, his single appointed task on earth, was his death on the cross as a 'sacrifice, oblation, and satisfaction for the sins of the whole world', as the Book of Common Prayer puts it. Everything else was just stage-management to make that possible. His birth, his teaching, his healings, his friendships, and the love he

13

gave and received – all this was simply the set on which the one single drama of his sacrificial death was to be acted out; mere incidentals to his great destiny.

Is this not a travesty of the gospel? Jesus was in one obvious sense a man of destiny: he was a man with a consistent and overarching purpose in his life. But 'destiny', as we have already seen, should not be taken to imply 'fate' or 'necessity'. The life we read about in the Gospels is not the life of someone swept along by his fate in such a way that it does not matter what damage is done on the way, so long as the one climax is reached. The Jesus of the Gospels does not strike us as in that sense less than human – like a character in a play who is there only as part of the mechanism of the plot, and whose role is finished once that task is achieved. Jesus strikes us as very human indeed, a man who responded to the detail and particularity of the setting in which he lived his life. His destiny, if that is indeed the right word, was not something that obliterated all the everyday activities of life, but a context which made them all take on a new importance. Jesus did not teach and heal and make friends in order to kill time, until it was time for the Romans to kill him. That is a dreadful trivialization of the life the Gospels record. He did all these things because there was no way of being God's love in our world except by being caught in the web of accidental encounters, the constraints of daily physical life, and the need for social and domestic life that belong inseparably to the human condition.

Jesus' life was not the unfolding of a prearranged set of events, all neatly shaped to point towards the passion. Indeed, the Gospels, for all their artistic structure, do not really give that impression. They are full of incidents that just happened, and could equally well have happened otherwise. There have been Christian schemes of thought which have seen the events of Jesus' life (and for that matter all the events in the history of the world) as foreordained by God, eliminating all chance and all randomness. But the Bible, taken by and large, does not support this way of thinking. The story it tells is full of muddle, inconsequential in places, and with surprises on every page; and the life of Jesus is no exception to this. Jesus was not speaking the lines of a script or obeying the directions of an invisible producer; he was living from day to day, just as we have to, with no certainty of what the future held – though undoubtedly with a foreboding that, if he insisted on sticking to the style of life and teaching to which he was committed, suffering and death could scarcely be avoided. That is a long way from saying starkly, 'Jesus was born to die.'

> Sometimes they strew his way,
> And his sweet praises sing;
> Resounding all the day
> Hosannas to their King.
> Then 'Crucify!'
> Is all their breath.
> And for his death
> They thirst and cry.

To live a human life means not to know for certain what each day will bring, still less what the end of it all will be. But the human vocation is to live through all these unpredictabilities with a consistent purpose and a consistent character, and that vocation Jesus, as we see him in the Gospels, embraced to the full. If we are right to see his life as the place where supremely God's own involvement in the world is to be found, then we might even say that God himself accepts the uncertainty and unpredictability of life and is prepared to live with it. Much of what happens in the world is arbitrary – natural disasters, social conditions which happen to have evolved in one way rather than another; and much is worse than arbitrary, it is the result of human malice and inconsistency. God's involvement with human life in Jesus is an acceptance of all this arbitrariness, not an act which sweeps it away and replaces it with a grand design leaving no room for error.

Perhaps it is not only in the life and death of Jesus that God submits to these constraints; perhaps, as I have hinted before, Jesus is principally the focal point where we see something that is true of God at all times and places and in all circumstances. God's control of the world he has made is not the tight control of someone driving a machine, but the loose control of a father or mother leaving their family room to develop freely. But God's 'family', in this comparison, does not mean only his human creatures, but everything he has made, including the physical world which also develops more like an organism than a machine, with room for randomness and accident. When natural disasters strike it is no *comfort* to the victims or to those who look on helplessly to say that such events are random and unintended by anyone – the result simply of the bad luck that comes from living in a world where

15

'accidents will happen'. But I sense that it is even less comforting to tell them that it is all part of a grand design, that God intended or even caused it, and that they should in some obscure sense be grateful for a painful death or a cruel bereavement. Christians do believe that the creation is not out of control by God; but the control is not so tight that accidents cannot occur, and a small accident on the cosmic scale of things can be enough to kill and maim thousands of people. 'I saw that under the sun the race is not to the swift, nor the battle to the strong, nor bread to the wise, nor riches to the intelligent, nor favour to the men of skill; but time and chance happen to them all' (Eccles. 9.11).

We may ask why God did not make a different sort of world, but we shall not get an answer. But instead we may ask a different question: is God indifferent to it all? And to that question Christianity *does* give an answer. No, he is not; he is caught up in the suffering himself, and knows from inside what it is like to be a victim of cruelty and arbitrariness. We do not see the meaning of Jesus' suffering and death if we try to understand it as a plan which God carried out by manipulating events in Galilee and Jerusalem two thousand years ago. We need instead to see that it could all have turned out differently. What God did in Jesus was not to pull all the strings himself, but to be on the receiving end of arbitrariness and unpredictability. The crowd which welcomed Jesus into Jerusalem might not have turned against him: it was not fated to do so.

Jesus did not get himself executed. The contingencies of expressing God's love for his people in the only way it could be expressed, in the very particular circumstances in which he happened to be, turned out to lead to collision with the authorities, and so to trial and execution. There was no 'must' about it, except the compulsion of divine love to be true to itself whatever happens. My colleague David Brown puts it like this:

> . . . note . . . the arbitrariness of the form of Jesus' death. Had he lived a few centuries earlier and lived in a different land it might have taken the relatively painless form of drinking hemlock, as with Socrates. Again, were it to have taken place this century in some of the countries of Latin America, it could well have been much more gruesome still – years of torture producing a wasted body that is finally just dumped in an anonymous grave . . . One might even be prepared to go further, and question whether the

story had to end brutally [at all]. For it is not so much the fact of
the suffering itself that produces its impact on us, as the way in
which Jesus responded to the diverse actors in the story as the
drama unfolded . . . God's involvement with suffering in Christ
is an involvement with that most frightening aspect of suffering,
its essential arbitrariness . . . It is this which makes Christ's cry
of dereliction from the cross the cry of all sufferers – Why me?
Why has God abandoned me to this fate? . . . Here in Jesus we
have God himself endorsing that cry, the tragic element in his
creation that each new sufferer must discover for himself, that
there is no reason why it has befallen him rather than another
. . . It is no part of the divine plan that any specific individual
suffer pain. But because pain is a tragic consequence of the
values the creation embodies, God has chosen to enter into our
pain at its most acute and now is always available to help
creatively transform whatever befalls us as one who knew pain at
its worst and potentially most destructive.[1]

Christians have not been good at grasping this 'arbitrariness' in
the story of their Lord's suffering and death – it has sounded too
much like saying that God was not in control. But unless we do
grasp it, we shall always run the risk of worshipping a God who did
not *quite* share our humanity, but always held something –
indeed, the most crucial thing – back. To put it in technical terms,
in Jesus the necessary and all-sufficient being of God accepts the
constraints of contingency, of living in a world where events turn
out in one way rather than another without anyone's being able to
predict or control them. What is divine is not the power to change
contingency into necessity: that is not the work of omnipotence, it is
a logical impossibility, and even God cannot do what is logically
impossible; as they were fond of saying in the Middle Ages, even
God cannot make a square circle. What is divine is the ability to live
contingent life in such a way that it becomes the place where the
divine word can speak and be heard by suffering humanity, itself
doomed to live through time and chance, accident and disaster and
defeat.

> The Word went forth,
>   Yet from his Father never went away,
> Came to his work on earth,
>   And laboured till the twilight of his day.

17

Men envied him: he went to death,
   By his own man betrayed,
Yet first to his own men himself had given
   In wine and broken bread.

In birth he gave himself a friend to men,
   At meat, their holy bread:
Dying, he gave himself their ransoming:
   Reigning, their high reward.

O Victim slain for us and our salvation,
   Opening the doors of light,
The warring hosts are set on our damnation,
   Give us the strength to fight.[2]

Christ our Victim,
whose beauty was disfigured
and whose body torn upon the cross;
open wide your arms
to embrace our tortured world,
that we may not turn away our eyes,
but abandon ourselves to your mercy.[3]

CHAPTER FOUR *God's Cross*

The word of the cross is folly to those who are perishing, but to us who are being saved it is the power of God. For it is written, 'I will destroy the wisdom of the wise, and the cleverness of the clever I will thwart.' Where is the wise man? Where is the scribe? Where is the debater of this age? Has not God made foolish the wisdom of the world? For since, in the wisdom of God, the world did not know God through wisdom, it pleased God through the folly of what we preach to save those who believe. For Jews demand signs and Greeks seek wisdom, but we preach Christ crucified, a stumbling block to Jews and folly to Gentiles, but to those who are called, both Jews and Greeks, Christ the power of God and the wisdom of God. For the foolishness of God is wiser than men, and the weakness of God is stronger than men.

1 Corinthians 1.18–25

In our Theology course in Oxford we have examinations in the Philosophy of Religion, the Psychology of Religion, and the Sociology of Religion. I've often wanted to introduce a further subject: the Pathology of Religion. For religion in various forms must have been the cause of almost unlimited misery in the world, and its pathological or diseased forms surely outnumber by far its healthy manifestations: Iran and Northern Ireland offer obvious examples, but there are many, many more.

Now of the pathological forms of religion that have been influential for Christians there are in particular two theories about human suffering that have a great deal to answer for in spreading misery among religious believers. The two theories are diametrically opposed, but that does not prevent some people from getting the benefit, or rather the harm, of believing in both at the same time. The first is the theory that all suffering is deserved, and is God's punishment for sin. And the second is the theory that suffering is a sign of being God's special favourite, chosen by him to suffer as a willing victim and so to embrace suffering as a joyful vocation. The two theories have this in common, that they do not see the removal of suffering as part of the will of God. Suffering is not seen as something scandalous, but on the contrary as something that has a

19

proper and God-given place in creation: either to punish the sinner, or to discipline and refine the righteous so that they may be God's agents in the world. And there is no doubt that there are parts of the Bible, and a great deal of Christian tradition, that support one or other of these beliefs.

Much of the history in the Old Testament is written to show that the people of Israel suffered because they deserved it; much of the New Testament, in St Paul's epistles and above all in 1 Peter, seems (at least taken at face value) designed to make Christians feel that they should embrace suffering voluntarily, because in doing so they, like Jesus before them, can bring salvation to humanity through their own pain. 'I rejoice in my sufferings for your sake, and in my flesh I complete what is lacking in Christ's afflictions for the sake of his body, that is, the church' (Col. 1.24); 'Rejoice in so far as you share Christ's sufferings . . . if one suffers as a Christian, let him not be ashamed, but under that name let him glorify God . . . let those who suffer according to God's will do right and entrust their souls to a faithful Creator' (1 Pet. 4.13–19). In later generations Christians sometimes sought martyrdom deliberately in order to take this imitation of Christ's sufferings to its logical conclusion. The second-century martyr St Ignatius of Antioch wrote feverishly to his friends asking them not to get him pardoned when he was under sentence of death, because his martyrdom was God's will. 'Here and now,' he wrote, 'as I write in the fullness of life, I am yearning for death with all the passion of a lover. Earthly longings have been crucified; in me there is left no spark of desire for the mundane things, but only a murmur of living water that whispers within me, "Come to the Father."'[1]

And yet I would still say that these ideas are in the end pathological; and you will search long and hard before you will find them in the teachings of Jesus. When told of the execution of some fellow Galileans by Pilate, Jesus commented, 'Do you think that these Galileans were worse sinners than all the other Galileans, because they suffered thus? . . . Or those eighteen upon whom the tower in Siloam fell and killed them, do you think that they were worse offenders than all the others who dwelt in Jerusalem?' (Luke 13.1–5). Of course not. When people asked him who had sinned, the blind man or his parents, that he should have been born blind, Jesus replied, 'Neither' (see John 9.3). Jesus rejected the idea that suffering is well-deserved divine punishment; and in nothing is this clearer than in his own healings. In the ancient world there were people (as there still are) who could heal others by means that medical science could not satisfactorily explain, and Jesus was clearly such a person; we do not even have to see his healing gifts as signs of divinity, for others could and can do similar things. But we can certainly see them as signs of his compassion for suffering humanity, and his refusal to accept any idea of suffering as God-given punishment.

Healing the sick was not, it seems, the primary concern of Jesus' ministry, for obviously he left far more people unhealed than he had time to heal; yet it was a natural part of it, almost as though healing just flowed out from him – indeed, in one story in the Gospels he does speak of it as a power that went out from him even without his deliberately intending it. (See Luke 8.42–8.) It is as though where Jesus was, God's will to heal and make whole sick and suffering people asserted itself spontaneously. Just as some people trail clouds of gloom with them, poisoning the air about them and making people feel hurt and injured, Jesus carried God's positive and health-giving power with him, bringing more exuberant life and making people flourish. The late Russell Harty in a memorable article once said that he divided the human race into radiators and drains;[2] and Jesus was undoubtedly a radiator, warming up the atmosphere wherever he was and bringing health to the sick in body and in mind.

But what about the other theory of suffering – the theory that God inflicts it on his specially chosen servants? Jesus' own suffering and death have been interpreted in this way; 'without shedding of blood there is no forgiveness of sins' (Heb. 9.22), and so Jesus had to die as a willing victim to bring life to others. As we have already seen, this makes Jesus' death sound pre-planned and foreordained, and fails to show how far it was arbitrary and unpredictable. Jesus' commitment was to his own life-giving message even if it brought death to himself, not to getting himself killed painfully because God wanted blood. His death was the result of human sin and callousness, not of divine planning. And Christians are to imitate Jesus in accepting the sufferings that come their way because they are loyal to Jesus' teachings and, like him, are committed to their fellow men and women; we are not supposed to go looking for sufferings to make us feel that we must be his disciples – because look how we are suffering! There is indeed a human vocation to do the will of God; there is no 'vocation' to suffering as such.

But, if only we can dig it out, there is a nugget of truth even in this most pathological of all religious theories, the glorification of suffering that has disfigured so much Christian teaching. The observation that those who are closest to God do tend to suffer is not a false one; and Christians have not been wrong in seeing a kind of inevitability in what happened to Jesus. Paradoxically, it was his very commitment to the life and health of others that made him attract such hatred and persecution and, eventually, betrayal and execution. As we read the stories in the Gospels, we can see that people found something provocative and offensive in the very acts of kindness and compassion which he kept performing; and we sense that this is more than an accident, that this style of goodness somehow always will attract hostility.

> Why, what hath my Lord done?
>   What makes this rage and spite?
> He made the lame to run,
>   He gave the blind their sight.
>   Sweet injuries!
>   Yet they at these
>   Themselves displease,
>   And 'gainst him rise.

Even if it were only a fictitious story, the Gospel narrative would show profound insight in the way it portrays human reactions to Jesus' healings – healings that were part of his refusal to regard human suffering as the punishment of sinners by an angry God. Only a rather naive person expects that conferring health and healing will bring gratitude and congratulation. Anyone who has lived many years in the world will not be surprised that instead it all too often brings hatred, envy, and suspicion.

People who heal others suffer for two reasons. First, they create obligations of gratitude; and few things are more painful for human beings than to feel indebted and obliged to someone else. Forgiveness in this respect is only an extreme case of healing. One of the hardest things in the world is to forgive someone for having forgiven you, for it at once makes them seem superior to you, it puts them in the right and you in some mysterious way in the wrong. When we harm someone, we set off a chain reaction which it is very difficult to stop. If they bear us a grudge, we are both injured, yet if they forgive us, we often resent it, and then they need to forgive us our resentment, and so it goes on. It takes two very big people to forgive and be forgiven, and to accept that the matter is really closed. The people Jesus healed or forgave were seldom up to their side of the bargain. And that is without counting the self-righteous people who could not bear to see others forgiven and accepted, of whom there were and always are an abundance. By doing good, Jesus made enemies; and that was not just accidentally so, it is part of the human condition that it should be so. In that sense it was indeed inevitable that he should suffer.

But there is an even more profound way in which healing brings suffering to the healer, and that is because much healing between two persons does involve the healer in taking the other person's pain into themselves. We may recoil (I believe we should recoil) from the idea that Jesus actually bore our sins in the sense of taking on himself the punishment due to us. But he did bear them in the sense that he felt the pain of those he had dealings with, by some kind of supreme empathy; and in a way the sufferings of the cross can be seen as a way of making literal and specific what was true in essence all through his ministry. When we say that in Jesus God himself bore the sins and pains of the world we are pointing to the truth that God too is a wounded healer. To heal is always and necessarily to feel pain, not to confer benefits without any suffering to oneself; and if this is necessarily true, then it is as true of God as it is of us. We cannot well imagine what it is for God himself to suffer pain, but we can imagine what it was for Jesus to do so, and Christian faith declares that one is a symbol and sign of the other. Helen Waddell put this better than anyone I have ever read in her novel *Peter Abelard*, written more than fifty years ago. In a famous passage Abelard and his servant, Thibault, find a rabbit caught in a trap:

> The rabbit stopped shrieking when they stooped over it, either from exhaustion, or in some last extremity of fear. Thibault held the teeth of the trap apart, and Abelard gathered up the little creature in his hands. It lay for a moment breathing quickly, then in some blind recognition of the kindness that had met it at the last, the small head thrust and nestled against his arm, and it died.

It was that last confiding thrust that broke Abelard's heart. He looked down at the little draggled body, his mouth shaking. 'Thibault,' he said, 'do you think there is a God at all? Whatever has come to me, I earned it. But what did this one do?'

Thibault nodded.

'I know,' he said. 'Only – I think God is in it too.'

Abelard looked up sharply.

'In it? Do you mean that it makes Him suffer, the way it does us?'

Again Thibault nodded.

'Then why doesn't he stop it?'

'I don't know,' said Thibault. 'Unless – unless it's like the Prodigal Son. I suppose the father could have kept him at home against his will. But what would have been the use? All this,' he stroked the limp body, 'is because of us. But all the time God suffers. More than we do.'

Abelard looked at him, perplexed . . .

'Thibault, do you mean Calvary?'

Thibault shook his head. 'That was only a piece of it – the piece that we saw – in time. Like that.' He pointed to a fallen tree beside them, sawn through the middle. 'That dark ring there, it goes up and down the whole length of the tree. But you only see it where it is cut across. That is what Christ's life was; the bit of God that we saw. And we think God is like that, because Christ was like that, kind, and forgiving sins and healing people. We think God is like that for ever, because it happened once, with Christ. But not the pain. Not the agony at the last. We think that stopped.'

Abelard looked at him, the blunt nose and the wide mouth, the honest troubled eyes . . .

'Then, Thibault,' he said slowly, 'you think that all this,' he looked down at the little quiet body in his arms, 'all the pain of the world, was Christ's cross?'

'God's cross,' said Thibault. 'And it goes on.'

'The Patripassian heresy,' murmured Abelard mechanically. 'But, O God, if it were true. Thibault, it must be. At least, there is something at the back of it that is true. And if we could find it – it would bring back the whole world.'[3]

How we can believe that God can and does suffer, without falling into some ancient heresy or other, I do not know either. This book is not a collection of theological definitions about the atonement or the passion, but an attempt to hint at 'something at the back of it that is true'. However we are to put it, we do believe if we are Christians that Christ's cross is not God causing someone else to suffer, but God himself at work to bear the sufferings of the world. What Abelard discovered was that this was not an isolated or extreme example of God's involvement in his suffering creation, but rather the typical and definitive case. The cross is not a momentary lapse or aberration on God's part; it is a single 'frame' from an infinite and infinitely consistent story, the story of how God takes all the pain of the world into himself. These are deep matters on which nothing we say is much better than childish babbling, but something like this is, perhaps, what St Paul calls the 'folly' of the cross, the foolishness of God which is wiser than all the wisdom of men.

Eternal Father,
your patience and mercy are without end:
permit us to carry the burdens of the heavy-laden
and to lay them on Christ
who has borne our griefs and carried our sorrows
and who makes all burdens light.[4]

CHAPTER FIVE

Christil Crucified

When I came to you, brethren, I did not come proclaiming to you the testimony of God in lofty words or wisdom. For I decided to know nothing among you except Jesus Christ and him crucified. And I was with you in weakness and in much fear and trembling; and my speech and my message were not in plausible words of wisdom, but in demonstration of the Spirit and power, that your faith might not rest in the wisdom of men but in the power of God.

Yet among the mature we do impart wisdom, although it is not a wisdom of this age or of the rulers of this age, who are doomed to pass away. But we impart a secret and hidden wisdom of God, which God decreed before the ages for our glorification. None of the rulers of this age understood this; for if they had, they would not have crucified the Lord of glory. But, as it is written, 'What no eye has seen, or ear heard, nor the heart of man conceived, what God has prepared for those who love him,' God has revealed to us through the Spirit.

1 Corinthians 2.1–10

Both the glorification of suffering and the assumption that it is always a punishment for sin represent diseased forms of religion. We have been trying to find our way to a healthier version of Christian faith – one that will avoid the superficial heartiness that simply ignores human pain, while yet not accounting for it in either of these pathological ways. But anyone who has begun to see the dreadful blind alleys down which religious faith has led people in their attempts to 'make sense' of suffering may be troubled by a suspicion that the worst has even yet not been told. What if religious faith is (as atheists suspect) *inherently* pathological? Might we not be better to abandon attempts to salvage something from the mess people have made of religion, and simply give it up completely? It isn't hard, after all, to find areas of conflict in the world today where religion seems essentially a destructive, even diabolical force. But on a smaller scale, in our own everyday lives, we frequently encounter the corrosive effects that strongly held religious beliefs can produce. Where there is disagreement about religion, tempers fray, abuse is hurled, charity dies: not for nothing are religion and politics often twinned as taboo subjects when people meet for a friendly meal or drink! And besides all this, there are all the people who are using religion as a drug or as a safety barrier between themselves and others: rejecting joy in the name of moral seriousness, making their own assurance of salvation into an excuse for being condescendingly superior to others, or covering their own stand-offishness or inadequacy with a cloak of religious discipline. Those who reject religion suspect religious people of hypocrisy and malice; and if we are honest, we should admit that religious observance does serve as a respectable garb for a multitude of human weaknesses and foibles. Sometimes I think that churches should carry a Government Health Warning: 'Religion can seriously damage your health.'

The convenient answer to all this is that there is bad religion and there is good religion, and it is important to be able to tell the difference. Of course this is quite true, so far as it goes; but it does ignore the possibility that being very 'religious' – being interested in religion and keen on practising it – might have an essential and in-built tendency to some of these characteristic failings. If the abuses of religion are so common and so unpleasant, might we not be better off without it altogether? Do the drawbacks simply outweigh the advantages? This may sound like a purely artificial question, to which in a few pages I am bound to answer 'no'; but I believe we should go a great deal further along the path towards the answer 'yes' than is altogether comfortable.

These thoughts are prompted by St Paul's words in 1 Corinthians: 'I decided to know nothing among you except Jesus Christ and him crucified'. The church to which Paul was writing was not, like some of the churches he had founded, inclined to be lax about practising its religion. On the contrary, it was full of people absolutely intoxicated by religious belief and practice, who loved their religion so much they couldn't get enough of it. They were rather like the Catholic apologist W.G. Ward, who once remarked that he would like to see a fresh papal bull, with a new infallible doctrine, published every morning in *The Times* to give him something new to believe in as he ate his breakfast. They thought that God was constantly revealing new truths, and they relished the opportunity to get their minds and their spiritual energies working on new religious ideas and practices – especially if, in the process, they could become more and more unlike the ignorant masses of the unenlightened they saw living all around them, some of whom seemed even to be invading the Church itself.

St Paul will have none of this. All such 'religion', he says, is mere human philosophy – 'philosophy' for him is a term of strong disapproval. It is nothing but people playing intellectual and spiritual games, turning God's self-revelation into a stick with which to beat others, a way of feeling distinguished from and superior to the rest of mankind. Such religion has as its main characteristic that it is *threatening*. It is a system with which we first frighten ourselves – thinking, 'Whatever will happen to me if I don't believe this or that doctrine, or if I don't perform this or that religious duty?' – and then frighten other people until they have come to share our own fears and run into the Church to seek shelter with us, on our terms. To put it in psychological terms: such religion is a neurosis. It is a pathological condition of self-induced fear, which we cure by submitting ourselves to complex religious rituals that then boost our own confidence and so give us a temporary relief. We huddle together with our fellow sufferers and keep up our morale by convincing ourselves that it is those outside who are the real sufferers.

St Paul's response to this kind of religion is indeed that, given the choice between it and no religion at all, it is better to have no religion at all. The heart of the gospel is not that mankind needs religion, but that mankind needs God; and the difference is utterly crucial. Religions at their best are only systems of belief and practice that we have devised to serve God, and if they induce fear, hatred, and pride, they are best dispensed with:

> Our little systems have their day;
>   They have their day and cease to be:
>   They are but broken lights of thee,
> And thou, O Lord, art more than they.[1]

The gospel, the good news comes when we abandon the search for a religion that will make us feel better, and come instead, in Paul's words, to know nothing but Jesus Christ *and him crucified*. It is not a threat but a promise. To preach Christ crucified, as Paul preached him, is not to tell people that unless they believe or do certain things, God will not love them; it is to pass on the good news that

God loves and saves and cares for us before we have done the slightest thing about it, simply because in Christ he accepts the world he has made and chooses to restore it (at cost to himself, not to us) to what he had originally meant it to be. To preach Christ crucified is not to issue a checklist of doctrines which you must tick and sign, not even a very short checklist: that is to use religion, however subtly, as a means of controlling others, making them insecure, wielding power over them. To preach Christ crucified is not to speak from a position of superiority, but to speak of the open-hearted love of God which values each of us highly enough to endure the cross for us – and to do it without wanting to induce in us feelings of unworthiness and self-hatred.

Of all the grotesque parodies of the meaning of the Lord's suffering and death few match that of F.W. Faber's (entirely well-intentioned!) hymn:

> Ever when tempted, make me see,
>   Beneath the olives' moon-pierced shade,
> My God, alone, outstretched, and bruised,
>   And bleeding, on the earth he made.
>
> And make me feel it was my sin,
>   As though no other sins there were,
> That was to him who bears the world,
>   A load that he could scarcely bear.[2]

Why, on this interpretation, did Jesus suffer? In order to make us realize how guilty we were to bring about his suffering. Thus, at a stroke, what Paul had seen as the *solution* to the problem of human sin – 'Christ crucified' – becomes the ultimate way of making the problem eternally insoluble. I have enough sins already, without Christ dying in order to provide me with the opportunity to commit another and infinite one, the sin of ingratitude for the sufferings he bore. Such interpretations of Christ crucified merely lock us yet more firmly inside the religious hall of mirrors, beyond any possibility of escape. To preach Christ crucified, however, is to proclaim that God has rescued us from all this self-absorption in sin and despair, and released us to give him thanks and praise as free men and women who no longer need their guilt. The gospel tells us that ' "what no eye has seen, nor ear heard, nor the heart of man conceived," God has revealed to us through the Spirit'; it speaks of what God has given us, not what preconditions he imposes. Like the father in the parable of the Prodigal Son, our Father runs to meet his children while they are still a long way off: 'God shows his love for us in that while we were yet sinners Christ died for us' (Rom. 5.8). Our religious practices are valuable only to the extent that they provide a channel through which we can express our joy and our response to the Father's love, revealed in Christ; beyond that, they are merely sophisticated forms of idolatry. The gospel is not threat, but promise; wherever God comes to meet us with his love, it is presented to us on a plate, and we have no more to do than stretch out our hands to receive it.

> Come, my Way, my Truth, my Life:
> Such a Way, as gives us breath:
> Such a Truth, as ends all strife:
> Such a Life, as killeth death.
>
> Come, my Light, my Feast, my Strength:
> Such a Light, as shows a feast:
> Such a Feast, as mends in length:
> Such a Strength, as makes his guest.
>
> Come, my Joy, my Love, my Heart:
> Such a Joy, as none can move:
> Such a Love, as none can part:
> Such a Heart, as joyes in love.[3]

> O God, before whose face
> we are not made righteous
> even by being right;
> free us from the need
> to justify ourselves
> by our own anxious striving,
> that we may be abandoned
> to faith in you alone,
> through Jesus Christ.[4]

CHAPTER SIX

Perfect Freedom

'I am the good shepherd; I know my own and my own know me, as the Father knows me and I know the Father; and I lay down my life for the sheep. And I have other sheep, that are not of this fold; I must bring them also, and they will heed my voice. So there shall be one flock, one shepherd. For this reason the Father loves me, because I lay down my life, that I may take it again. No one takes it from me, but I lay it down of my own accord. I have power to lay it down, and I have power to take it again; this charge I have received from my Father.'

John 10.14–18

St John's Gospel is of all the Gospels the one which stresses this theme: that Jesus was the master of his own fate. He is presented as a figure who knew no uncertainty and no weakness, and who controlled his own destiny. In the garden of Gethsemane he was taken only because he chose to be taken; he himself had given the sop of bread to Judas, marking him out as the predestined traitor; and when Judas had gone out into the night to accomplish the betrayal, he told the other disciples, 'Now is the Son of man glorified' (John 13.31): the cross, where he would triumph over the evil world, was now a certainty.

To a modern person this way of presenting Jesus smacks too much of an idea I have already called in question in this book: the idea of Jesus as the stage-manager of his own execution. We can understand why the evangelist wanted to make it plain that Jesus' fate did not overtake him without the providence of God, that it was not a mere accident of history, but the climax of a great purpose. For this reason he told the story of Jesus so as to stress that he was not swept along by forces beyond his control, but held the threads of his destiny in his own hands, where God had placed them. But the price of seeing it like this is to remove our own feeling of solidarity with Jesus. It makes him utterly unlike us, frail human beings who really are at the mercy of forces beyond our own control. And surely it is essential to our faith to believe that in Jesus God himself actually released his hold on the threads of destiny, and submitted to just that random and meaningless pressure of forces beyond anyone's control which is what we mean by human history. The Jesus who is our Saviour and Friend is not a majestic figure who can fix even the time of his own death. On the contrary, he is a person who suffered the very worst that life can bring, the experience of the anguish that belongs to mindless and casual pain, the experience of being not an agent but a patient – that is, a victim, a person at other people's disposal and with no control whatever over his own fate.[1] That is the hell into which Christ descended. It is a travesty to present him as a calm philosophical figure fixing his own destiny.

Yet St John's Gospel is not wrong to present Jesus' suffering as a matter of his own free choice, and to see him as mysteriously in control of all that happened to him. Jesus' freedom is not a matter of his having arranged and orchestrated his own death, like a flamboyant suicide. It is a freedom of a far more profound kind than that. This can be understood better if we set Jesus in his historical context.

In the ancient world, very much as in most parts even of the modern world, people were acutely aware of the shortness of human life and of how fragile the human lot was. The Roman Empire contained a small élite of free citizens who were also rich enough to have some control over their own careers, marriages, homes, and lives – provided diseases and natural accidents didn't intervene; but the vast mass of mankind had no choice in any of these matters. Philosophers, faced with this obvious and burdensome lack of freedom in most of the human race, asked what freedom was nevertheless available to mankind; and they found the answer in a certain way of developing the character. The truly free man, it was said, was not the person who had the wealth and leisure to organize his own life, but the person whose inner resources enabled him to cope with whatever chances and hardships life threw in his path.

The best representative of this way of thinking is the philosophy called Stoicism, which has given us the modern word 'stoic' for a person who persists with resignation in difficult circumstances. Stoics believed that the person with the right inner attitudes was free whatever might happen to him from outside; virtue was its own reward. There are faint echoes of this sense in the moving accounts one sometimes reads of people in concentration camps in Nazi Germany or Stalinist Russia whose inner freedom was such that they could actually pity their gaolers, seeing them as poor dupes and victims of the system while they, the prisoners, were free because they refused to be deprived of their own sense of human dignity by whatever dehumanizing cruelty was heaped on them.

> He who has made his reckoning with life
> Hath haughty fate beneath his feet,
> And gazing straight at fortune, good or ill,
> Can hold a high indomitable head . . .
>
> Why do unhappy folk eye with such awe
> Fierce tyrants with no sinews in their rage?
> Have done with hope and fear
> And you've disarmed him: he is impotent.[2]

Jesus' freedom, his control of his own destiny, was of a kind related to this. Judas could betray him, but Judas was a pawn in someone else's game, driven to despair by his own treachery and greed and self-loathing. Caiaphas could hand him over to the Romans, but Caiaphas did so because he was afraid, afraid of the disturbing message of divine love which Jesus had preached. Pilate could order his execution, but Pilate was a fool who did not even know the answer to his own question, 'What is truth?' The helpless figure at the centre of all this could do nothing to save himself; yet his integrity was his freedom, and nothing could take that freedom from him.

But Jesus was more than a Stoic philosopher. In him we do not see the integrity and self-composure of the person with an iron will and a proper sense of his own dignity, who can afford to despise even his torturers. That kind of person is deeply admirable, and is far greater than most people have it in them to be. But Jesus' greatness is not precisely of that kind. Jesus' freedom is expressed not in detachment and austere contempt for his murderers, but in love and compassion for them, even for them, especially for them:

> They rise, and needs will have
>   My dear Lord made away;
> A murderer they save,
>   The Prince of Life they slay.
>   Yet cheerful he

35

> To suffering goes,
> That he *his foes*
> From thence might free.

The Stoic sage is a person whose ability to rise above his suffering is godlike, because he can be completely detached even in agony. Jesus is not like that; detachment is the last thing we associate with him, and he does not look down on his torturers and murderers, but dies to save them. But it is precisely in this that Christians see Jesus as godlike, indeed as the visible expression of God himself. And to believe in Jesus as the embodiment of God is to change radically what we mean by God. The God revealed is Jesus is not a detached God, but one whose own freedom is his boundless ability to commit himself to the needs of the world he has made.

We say all too glibly that we believe in a God of love; but we do not always stop to consider what this implies. It implies that Jesus is the perfect symbol or icon of the God we believe in: the person whose self-fulfilment, and therefore whose ultimate freedom, lies in putting himself under the heavy yoke of being at the disposal of human beings, with all their pent-up 'envy, hatred, and malice, and all uncharitableness'. The ultimate freedom is the freedom to give oneself away to someone else. Jesus is the living symbol of a God who embraces that freedom gladly, and who gives himself away for the sake of the people he has made.

The signs of that self-giving love are offered to us every time Christians celebrate the Eucharist, when they recall the meal at which the Lord, having loved his own who were in the world, loved them to the utmost extent. The broken bread and wine poured out are symbols of the total self-emptying and brokenness of the one who freely laid down his life because he freely embraced the lot of the whole human race, including – including above all – its helplessness and bondage to death and suffering. That is the kind of God to whom all who take his body and blood in the Eucharist are committing themselves; a God who will 'break his own heart to comfort ours',[3] and who offers us the chance to become people who will do the same for each other and, indeed, for the least of our brothers and sisters. It is enough to make you hesitate before holding out your hands to take the Lord's body and blood; and yet the hesitation should be only momentary, for, true to himself, God gives us himself without strings, and nourishes in us the ability to follow him, not through threats and terror, but through love and pity.

> Philosophers have measur'd mountains,
> Fathom'd the depths of seas, of states, and kings,
> Walk'd with a staffe to heav'n, and tracèd fountains:
>   But there are two vast, spacious things,
> The which to measure it doth more behove:
> Yet few there are that sound them; Sinne and Love.
>
> Who would know Sinne, let him repair
> Unto Mount Olivet; there shall he see
> A man so wrung with pain, that all his hair,
>   His skin, his garments bloudie be.
> Sinne is that presse and vice, which forceth pain
> To hunt his cruell food through ev'ry vein.
>
> Who knows not Love, let him assay
> And taste that juice, which on the crosse a pike
> Did set again abroach; then let him say
>   If ever he did taste the like.
> Love is that liquor sweet and most divine,
> Which my God feels as bloud; but I, as wine.[4]

Christ our teacher,
you urge us beyond all reason
to love our enemies,
and pray for our oppressors.
May we embrace such folly
not through subservience, but strength;
that unmeasured generosity
may be poured into our lap,
through Jesus Christ.[5]

CHAPTER SEVEN

Down into Silence

Then Jesus, crying with a loud voice, said, 'Father, into thy hands I commit my spirit!' And having said this he breathed his last. Now when the centurion saw what had taken place, he praised God, and said, 'Certainly this man was innocent!' And all the multitudes who assembled to see the sight, when they saw what had taken place, returned home beating their breasts. And all his acquaintances and the women who had followed him from Galilee stood at a distance and saw these things.

Now there was a man named Joseph from the Jewish town of Arimathea. He was a member of the council, a good and righteous man, who had not consented to their purpose and deed, and he was looking for the kingdom of God. This man went to Pilate and asked for the body of Jesus. Then he took it down and wrapped it in a linen shroud, and laid him in a rock-hewn tomb, where no one had ever yet been laid. It was the day of Preparation, and the sabbath was beginning. The women who had come with him from Galilee followed, and saw the tomb, and how his body was laid; then they returned, and prepared spices and ointments.

On the sabbath day they rested according to the commandment.

Luke 23.46–56

One very cold and blustery Good Friday I emerged from church in the afternoon to find that the wind had dropped. When I commented casually on this, an old lady in the congregation said, 'Oh, it always does; it's always quiet after three o'clock on Good Friday.' Superstition or old wives' tale, of course; yet a faithful reflection of the atmosphere that lasted from Jesus' death until the moment – the moment whose time we do not know, and which no Gospel records – of the resurrection. As the Psalm says, 'The earth trembled, and was still, when God arose to establish judgement' (Ps. 76.8–9). Good Friday afternoon and the Saturday that follows are an empty space, silence and quiet after the pain and the storm; the space in which the disciples huddled together to get what comfort they could from each other, and from knowing that their Master was no longer suffering. Their sole concern was the concern that unites people across the centuries, from the most primitive men and women of whom we have records up to the relatives of those who die today through accident, violence, or natural disaster: the concern that the dead should have decent burial. So they busied themselves preparing spices for anointing the body and giving it some of the repose of peaceful death; though a moment's thought will remind us that it was by now no more than a mangled and distorted carcase after whips, thorns, nails and, no doubt, vultures had finished with it.

Burial is supremely the act by which we seek to humanize death and to shake our fist at the fate that is the lot of all human beings – as though we could deny the truth we all know in our heart, that through death we are utterly separated even from those with whom our lives have been joined at the profoundest level. The body which we have loved and cherished turns before our eyes into a mere inanimate object. Good Friday confirms what we read in Genesis but somehow never believe, that we are dust, and to dust we shall return. Jesus goes, as all of us will go, down the solitary path to the grave, where no one can accompany us, and disappears into nothingness, into the shadowy world where the Old Testament chillingly tells us that even the praises of God are silenced, and fellowship with him is lost. 'The dead do not praise the LORD, nor do any that go down into silence' (Ps. 115.17).

Jesus had been abandoned by his followers even before his trial: 'You will all fall away because of me this night; for it is written, "I will smite the shepherd, and the sheep of the flock will be scattered"' (Matt. 26.31). But in death he abandoned them, as we all must abandon those we love. No one who is bereaved does not feel resentment – and then guilt because of the injustice of the resentment – against the one who has gone away and left them. And especially so, perhaps, when they know the death could have been avoided, as Jesus' could have been. He didn't have to move into the public eye when he could have remained an obscure carpenter, to choose a disciple who couldn't be trusted, to go to Jerusalem when he could have stayed in Galilee, to bait and exasperate the authorities. He was, obviously, a highly social and gregarious person, but he had chosen a course that led inevitably to isolation and then to solitary death, and now he lay, in the words of Psalm 88.5, 'like one forsaken among the dead, like the slain that lie in the grave, like those whom thou dost remember no more, for they are cut off from thy hand'. The only comfort to be had, in the face of the abyss of nothingness that lies before all who remember that they must one day go the same way, is the comfort of anaesthesia – the hope that the wind will drop, and that empty silence will at least bring an end of pain and suffering. So they prepared the spices and ointments, and rested on the sabbath according to the commandment.

When we say in the creed that Jesus 'suffered death, and was buried', we are saying that he did not dodge this universal human experience. The resurrection which Christians believe has already occurred for him, and for which they hope for themselves, is not a process by which death and burial are somehow miraculously left out, and Jesus slips magically from earthly life to life everlasting. His path led down into the depths, and passed through the experience of total isolation and loneliness which is the fear clutching at all human hearts. What we see in him is not a superman who cheated death, but a man like ourselves. As his followers we are not his fan club, pretending he is immune from the trials that beset us. On the contrary, we follow him because we see him as someone who shares with us even that worst fear of all, the fear of being alone and abandoned not only by friends and family but by God himself – someone, therefore, whom we are allowed to love and pity as we hope that others may love and pity us when we come to our own end in loneliness and isolation. Jesus' grave is not the monument of a superhuman figure, as the ridiculous tombs of dictators claim so foolishly to be: it is our grave, the insignificant and dusty place to which we all must come.

> In life, no house, no home,
>   My Lord on earth might have;
> In death, no friendly tomb,
>   But what a stranger gave.
>   What may I say?
>   Heav'n was his home;
>   But mine the tomb
>   Wherein he lay.

Christians don't spend Good Friday in misery, because for us the Lord's resurrection is a reality; as the Psalmist says, sorrow may abide for a night's stay, but joy comes in the morning (Ps. 30.5). Yet his death was our death, and to rise with him we too have to pass through the grave and gate of death. And if there is a time to laugh, there is also a time to weep, and the Christian who has not learned to weep still has much else to learn. The route which God took to deliver us from eternal death was a very roundabout route, not the way of power and domination but the way of suffering and weakness; and so the way from Good Friday to Easter lies through the valley of the shadow. A God who simply annihilated all human suffering would of course greatly relieve our fears and soothe our sorrows, but only a God who chooses to save us by passing through the same experiences himself can break our hearts.

It is no superficial God who chooses the way of the cross and who lies in the grave, sharing the horror and emptiness that come to all things human; and the joy of the resurrection is no superficial joy, not the careless cheerfulness of children but the deep joy of adults who have passed through bitter suffering and come through to a new depth of vision. The faces of the angels, perhaps we may guess, are smooth and unwrinkled, glowing with simple pleasure in the goodness of the creation; sin and suffering to them are a distant dream, guessed at but never experienced. But the typical Christian face is deeply lined with the pain and sorrow of the world, though the lines have turned to laughter-lines through the resurrection which brought Christ up even from the depths of the pit, where God is not, and restored him to undying life. Christian joy has little to do with broad, innocent grins; it comes through sharing in Christ's sufferings and death, and so becoming like the risen Christ himself, who for the joy that was set before him had endured the cross, despising the shame. Christians share Christ's victory through sharing his lonely vocation to be the love of God for a fallen world, and like him going out to embody God whatever the cost.

> Alone to sacrifice thou goest, Lord,
>> Giving thyself to death whom thou hast slain.
> For us thy wretched folk is any word,
> > Who know that for our sins this is thy pain?
>
> For they are ours, O Lord, our deeds, our deeds,
> > Why must thou suffer torture for our sin?
> Let our heart suffer for thy passion, Lord,
> > That sheer compassion may thy mercy win.

This is that night of tears, the three days' space,
    Sorrow abiding of the eventide,
Until the day break with the risen Christ,
    And hearts that sorrow shall be satisfied.

So may our hearts have pity on thee, Lord,
    That they may sharers of thy glory be:
Heavy with weeping may the three days pass,
    To win the laughter of thine Easter Day.[1]

Christ, whose bitter agony
was watched from afar by women,
enable us to follow the example
of their persistent love;
that, being steadfast in the face of horror,
we may also know the place of resurrection,
in your name.[2]

CHAPTER EIGHT

The Stranger

Christ has been raised from the dead, the first fruits of those who have fallen asleep. For as by a man came death, by a man has come also the resurrection of the dead. For as in Adam all die, so also in Christ shall all be made alive. But each in his own order: Christ the first fruits, then at his coming those who belong to Christ. Then comes the end, when he delivers the kingdom to God the Father after destroying every rule and every authority and power. For he must reign until he has put all his enemies under his feet. The last enemy to be destroyed is death. 'For God has put all things in subjection under his feet.' But when it says, 'All things are put in subjection under him,' it is plain that he is excepted who put all things under him. When all things are subjected to him, then the Son himself will also be subjected to him who put all things under him, that God may be everything to every one.

1 Corinthians 15.20–28

In the Gospel stories about Jesus' appearances after his resurrection there is a persistent and puzzling theme: that the disciples did not recognize him. In the garden, at first light, Mary Magdalene thought he was the gardener. It was only when he called her by name that she knew him (John 20.16). On the road to Emmaus the disciples were with him for a long part of their journey, and in the inn with him right up until the meal was served; it was only when he took the bread and gave thanks that they recognized him, and could ask – wise after the event – 'Did not our hearts burn within us while he talked to us on the road, while he opened to us the scriptures?' (Luke 24.32). By the lakeside, it was only his supernatural knowledge of where they should cast their nets for a catch that made the beloved disciple cry out, 'It is the Lord!' (John 21.7). Through all these mysterious accounts there is this common thread: the risen Christ, it seems, was not immediately recognizable. Thomas doubted because he had not seen him; but the other disciples were scarcely easier to convince. They were in no doubt that there was really someone there; but who was it? Was the mysterious stranger in fact Jesus, or was he an impostor, or a ghost, or an angel, or even some-

45

one with merely a slight superficial, accidental resemblance to Jesus?

The stories about the resurrection appearances are mysterious indeed, and have depths that scholars despair of sounding. But all of them are alike in this, that the crucial moment in them is not the moment of vision, but the moment of recognition. Contrary to what is common in many other accounts that have come down to us of holy visions, the disciples don't suddenly 'see Jesus' in the sense that they immediately say, 'Look, surely that's Jesus.' They see simply a man, who could be anyone. The crucial moment is the moment when they recognize him – and at that moment, paradoxically, he vanishes from their sight or (as with Mary in the garden) refuses to allow them to hold on to him. Once he is recognized, he departs swiftly. We may of course not believe in the stories, but at least we should recognize that they are very unlike accounts of hallucinations; nor do they reflect the kind of fleeting glimpses people often catch of those they have loved during the first few days or weeks after their death. I don't know how we are to explain those very common experiences, but they are certainly not the same as the kind of experience the disciples are said to have had, in which they spent a considerable time with someone, talked to him, even ate with him, and only at the end realized that the person they had been with was Jesus himself – none other than the Master they had known for so long, and thought they had lost irretrievably.

Lost, at least, until God should raise all the righteous at the last day. For of course these were people who believed that resurrection was entirely possible, and in fact that at the end of time it would happen to everyone, Jesus included. What they could not believe was that Jesus or anyone else could be raised to life again *now*, in ordinary time. Whoever the interesting stranger in the garden or on the road or by the lake might be, he could not therefore be Jesus, for the end of time had not yet come, and Jesus must still be dead. The disciples had indeed hoped that the great deliverance of Israel at the end of time was dawning, in Jesus' life and ministry: 'The kingdom of God is at hand,' he had proclaimed. But Jesus had been supposed to be God's agent to usher in this great deliverance, and obviously he had failed to do so, dying the ultimate God-forsaken death of the cross. The last days had obviously not arrived; so the stranger, whoever else he might be, could not be Jesus.

But then the stranger spoke a word, or performed an action, that had his unmistakable mark on it. Scales fell from the eyes, the light dawned; it could be no one else. Because the kingdom of God had not dawned, they had assumed, the stranger could not be Jesus; even if he looked like him (and apparently, he didn't, much), it must be wishful thinking. It could not be him; yet it was. And if so, then what followed? No one could be raised from the dead unless the kingdom of God had dawned. But here he was, alive again. So the unthinkable was the only possibility, that the kingdom of God had indeed arrived. All the other manifestations of the resurrection – especially an empty tomb – could have a range of explanations. But a meeting with Jesus who had been dead but was now alive could mean only one thing: that God had begun to raise the dead; that the kingdom was here and now; that the winter and the night were over, and dawn and spring had arrived.

For the first Christians the association between Jesus' resurrection and the dawning of God's kingdom was integral to their whole way of thinking: Jesus, as St Paul puts it, was the 'first fruits of those who have fallen asleep' – like the first sheaf in the harvest. And it was in recognizing the first person to be raised from the dead as Jesus and no one else that people saw clearly of what nature God's kingdom really was. The values for which Jesus stood, and which led him to his death when he would not abandon them, were values of peace, joy, and self-sacrifice: self-giving love was the hallmark of all he did and taught. If Jesus, and no one else, is the first person whom God raised from the dead, then these are the values that God shares with us. God is on the same side as Jesus and agrees with us that someone like Jesus is the ultimate example of what human beings can and should be.

To say that God can and will raise the dead, however hard it is for us to believe, was not news to first-century Palestinian Jews: many, perhaps most people believed that. To say that God had now already raised a dead man to life was startling news indeed, and it indicated that he was inaugurating a new world. But that was still not enough; it mattered desperately who this man was. The Christian gospel was and is the good news that it is *Jesus* whom God raised from the dead, 'this Jesus whom you crucified', as Peter told the crowd on the day of Pentecost (Acts 2.36).

> Here might I stay and sing.
>   No story so divine;
> Never was love, dear King,

Never was grief like thine!
This is my Friend,
   In whose sweet praise
   I all my days
Could gladly spend.

So the resurrection of Jesus is not just a cancelling of the past, an obliteration of the sorry story of suffering and conflict and bitter death. Jesus' past is taken up into his resurrection.[1] The Lord who, as Paul puts it, is 'seated at the right hand of God' (Col. 3.1), is the same Jesus, and still bears the marks of the nails. The kingdom of God which Christ's resurrection inaugurates is not a realm in which Christians forget what he was like in his earthly life, triumph vindictively over their enemies, and turn the tables on those who persecuted and killed their Lord. It is a kingdom where the values which led that Lord to accept suffering at the hands of his own creatures are reaffirmed for all eternity.

When Christ came from the shadows by the stream
   Of Phlegethon,
Scars were upon his feet, his hands, his side.
   Not, as dulled souls might deem,
   That he, who had the power
Of healing all the wounds whereof men died,
   Could not have healed his own,
But that those scars had some divinity,
   Carriage of mystery,
Life's source to bear the stigmata of Death . . .

By these same scars, in prayer for all mankind,
   Before his Father's face,
He pleads our wounds within his mortal flesh,
And all the travail of his mortal days:
   For ever interceding for His grace,
   Remembering where forgetfulness were blind,
   For ever pitiful, for ever kind,
Instant that Godhead should take thought for man,
   Remembering the manhood of His Son,
   His only Son, and the deep wounds he bore.

By these same scars his folk will not give o'er
   Office of worship, whilst they see,
     Passion, thy mystery:
   In those dark wounds their weal,
In that descent to hell their climb to the stars,
     His death, their life,
   Their wreath, his crown of thorns.[2]

Our own resurrection, which begins, Christians believe, in the present life, does not mean that all the sufferings we ourselves may have undergone, all the troubles we have known, all the disappointments we have experienced, are simply wiped out as though they had never been, and we are turned into angels playing harps on clouds. Resurrection for each of us means that God affirms what we have become, with all the suffering that has made us the people we are, and builds it all into the character he stamps upon us as he raises us to new life with him. Resurrection means that God does not obliterate our past, but integrates it into his new order. Christians celebrate at Easter the beginning of new life in Christ; yet it is a new life in which they still recognize the selves they have been, just as the disciples recognized the Jesus they had known, transformed and healed yet still the same, the same yesterday, today, and for ever.

God of terror and joy,
you arise to shake the earth.
Open our graves
and give us back the past;
so that all that has been buried
may be freed and forgiven,
and our lives may return to you
through the risen Christ.[3]

CHAPTER NINE *Christian Names*

But Mary stood weeping outside the tomb, and as she wept she stooped to look into the tomb; and she saw two angels in white, sitting where the body of Jesus had lain, one at the head and one at the feet. They said to her, 'Woman, why are you weeping?' She said to them, 'Because they have taken away my Lord, and I do not know where they have laid him.' Saying this, she turned round and saw Jesus standing, but she did not know that it was Jesus. Jesus said to her, 'Woman, why are you weeping? Whom do you seek?' Supposing him to be the gardener, she said to him, 'Sir, if you have carried him away, tell me where you have laid him, and I will take him away.' Jesus said to her, 'Mary.' She turned and said to him in Hebrew, 'Rabboni!' (which means Teacher). Jesus said to her, 'Do not hold me, for I have not yet ascended to the Father; but go to my brethren and say to them, I am ascending to my Father and your Father, to my God and your God.'

John 20.11–17

What's in a name? Everything and nothing. At first our names are arbitrary – mere tags that distinguish us from each other. Yet as we grow and develop our name becomes a point round which associations cluster, till to change it is a major decision, involving us in deliberately jettisoning something of what we have become. A person's name, repeated by someone who loves them, will sometimes penetrate the darkness of coma and stir a murmur of recognition from someone near to death. There is no incident in the Gospels that catches at my throat as much as the moment in the garden, when Jesus reveals his identity not by speaking his own name but by addressing Mary Magdalene by hers, and she stirs, and turns, and recognizes him. All that she is seems focused in her name, all Jesus' love and concern for her is narrowed to this single point; and as he speaks her name, she is identified and welcomed, affirmed and cherished. At the beginning of creation, we read in Genesis, God spoke the name of each thing he was making, and so it came to be: in the laconic Hebrew of Genesis we read, 'God said, Be light! and light was.' The risen Christ recreates the world, beginning with those he loved most, and does so by naming them. As he does so, he recalls all that they are and have been, and gives it his blessing, and they become part of his new kingdom, called by name and so recognized and confirmed in being.

A few years ago the massive German made-for-television saga *Heimat* was shown in Britain, and like many others I spent every evening for a week glued to the television set. It told the story of a family living in Germany in the Hunsrück, west of the Rhine near the border with Luxemburg, from the end of the First World War down to the 1980s. The story was focused by being seen through the eyes of another Mary, Maria, who was a child in the first episode and whose death and funeral brought the whole cycle to its conclusion. Put like that, it sounds like a German version of Galsworthy's *The Forsyte Saga*, memorably adapted in the last days of black-and-white television; and, indeed, some people regarded it as really no more than a very high-class soap opera. But no tale of life in Germany over that particular period could have the simplicity and comparative blandness of that kind of English family saga. *Heimat* had the serious task of telling the story of a German village through the Nazi period, the Second World War, and the post-War reconstruction and prosperity of modern Germany, and of doing so in such a way that Germans watching it would be enabled at last to make some kind of peace with their past. And not a facile peace; the film did not encourage anyone to disclaim responsibility for the terrible events of this century, but acknowledged them with honesty. Yet the honesty was not negative or destructive, not a way of torturing oneself with the past as in so much that is said about the Nazi years in modern Germany – or so it seems to me, as an occasional visitor and one who loves what Germany has now become. The honesty in *Heimat* did not spare its German audience, and yet it held out (or so I thought) a promise of genuinely new life: the possibility that it could once again become permissible to be German, and to be glad of it – not at all in the old nationalistic way which led to such appalling suffering for others, but in quietness and humility.

This theme, never made explicit but always present for those with eyes to see, came to fulfilment in the final scenes. The dying Maria sees herself once again as the young girl we first met, in a room surrounded by all the people she has known and loved; and she simply turns to each one in turn, looks into their eyes, and says their name. You might think that this would sound monotonous, like the reading of a roll of honour, but once you have lived through the film, you realize that it is the one thing that is needed to make each of the characters live again; to make the whole life of each one part of something larger which is being affirmed and brought to completion. I have never seen the power of names revealed with such force. Indeed, since seeing *Heimat* I feel quite differently about the ritual reading of names, and no longer see that as in any sense an empty act. Maria speaks each name, and looks into the person's eyes; and that person stands before us as a whole, in each phase of their life, in their good deeds and their bad, for better, for worse, in sickness and in health. We see that whoever they were, and whatever they did, they were somehow necessary to the whole story.

The naming of the characters in this scene from a remarkable film is, like the scene at dawn in the garden, about resurrection. Maria's role in naming each one, and so assigning them a place in the story and releasing them from the threat of futility and pointlessness, is an act of what is now sometimes called healing the memories.[1] It asserts that what is past cannot be changed or undone, yet can be redeemed. Omar Khayyám says that

> The Moving Finger writes; and, having writ,
> Moves on: nor all thy Piety nor Wit
> Shall lure it back to cancel half a Line,
> Nor all thy Tears wash out a Word of it.[2]

The past stands fixed in letters of blood, and we must face it. But the message of *Heimat* – which is also the message of the garden – is that even the past is in the hands of God. Even he cannot rewrite it, but he can transform it. The risen Christ is still the crucified Christ; his pain cannot be cancelled or forgotten while heaven and earth remain. But God's power to give new life is unlimited, and even pain – what is more, even the guilt of having caused pain – are not beyond his healing touch. The forgiveness and reconciliation of which the naming scene in *Heimat* speaks are the prerogative of divine love alone, for only God can bring life out of the absolute deadness of evils such as those that disfigure the history of Europe in our time. But the scene in the garden speaks of the same divine power available for each of us, as the risen Christ speaks our name

53

and calls us from the nothingness – or, worse, the evil – of our past into a future where even the person we have been can be mysteriously salvaged and reaffirmed.

Resurrection is the fulfilment of the promise in the book of Isaiah: 'Fear not, for I have redeemed you; I have called you by name, you are mine' (Isa. 43.1). Christ is risen, and we are risen with him, because he has called us each by name and refused to let us be dragged down by our past, whatever it may be, into the pit of death and annihilation. Indeed, the new life in Christ fulfils also the promise of Revelation: 'To him who conquers I will give some of the hidden manna, and I will give him a white stone, with a new name written on the stone which no one knows except him who receives it' (Rev. 2.17). A new start is what God gives us, and this might well be called 'a new name'. But when the mystery of the new name is revealed it will turn out, I think, that it is our old name all the time. God will give us back ourselves, transformed but not destroyed, and will allow us to possess all our yesterdays as a part of what we have become. Like Mary Magdalene's, our past probably does not bear close inspection; yet, like her, we are called by name by the risen Christ, reaffirmed in all our individuality, and restored as daughters and sons of the living God.

Christ our healer,
beloved and remembered by women,
speak to the grief which makes us forget,
and the terror that makes us cling,
and give us back our name;
that we may greet you clearly,
and proclaim your risen life.[3]

CHAPTER TEN

The Death of Death

> If then you have been raised with Christ, seek the things that are
> above, where Christ is, seated at the right hand of God. Set your
> minds on things that are above, not on things that are on earth.
> For you have died, and your life is hid with Christ in God. When
> Christ who is our life appears, then you also will appear with him
> in glory.
>
> Colossians 3.1–4

A local radio station decided to run a series of programmes on
religion, with various local clergy providing the basic material, a
certain number of recorded interviews to add depth, and a few
'experts' called in to make comments and respond to phone-ins.
The 'syllabus' was very carefully drafted, and covered all aspects of
the Christian faith and its relation to other faiths. Late in the day,
however, the producer decided that a trailer was needed to capture
people's interest. So he devised a short programme on the
paranormal, with discussions of ghosts, out-of-the-body experiences,
and exorcism – to explore, as he put it, points of contact 'between
the abstract theology of the main series and the point where religion
really impinges on ordinary people's lives'.

It is easy to imagine how this was received by those who had
been asked to take part in the series. Christians do not want to have
their faith discussed as if it were all about what might be called the
'spooky'. But no doubt the producer had done his homework; he
knew that this is one important area of misunderstanding between
Christians and non-Christians. Those inside the Christian religion
perceive it sometimes as exciting, enriching, demanding; sometimes,
no doubt, as dull, prosaic, even a chore; but hardly ever as occult,
weird, or paranormal. But outside observers frequently see
something arcane about Christian services and rites, and feel the
distinction between religion on the one hand and magic, superstition,
and mystery on the other as much finer than Christians suppose.
Every clergyman has encountered people who have had little
contact with Christianity and for whom a church is a very
frightening place, the sanctuary and altar no less terrifying than a
site where black magic is practised. And resurrection – the

resurrection of Jesus, and the resurrection which Christians await for themselves and for all mankind – is supremely a subject on which mutual incomprehension reigns. It is hard for Christians to realize how much the Gospels read like ghost stories; and how little this seems to matter.

I first understood what a gulf there is between 'official' Christian thought and the common-sense views of many people when I preached a sermon on the *uniqueness* of Jesus' resurrection one Easter Day. I was trying to stress – as a Christian preacher must – that the Lord's resurrection was not just an interesting incident in the past which *happened* never to have occurred before or since, but a radical break with past history. Furthermore (I said) what matters is not just that Jesus actually rose from the dead – important as that is – but that this was an event with a certain depth of meaning in it. It meant that God himself was endorsing the kind of life Jesus had led (a point made above, in chapter 9). Therefore it was crucial that it was Jesus who rose to new life rather than (say) Pontius Pilate or Judas Iscariot: 'this Jesus whom you crucified'. In other words, Jesus' resurrection is not simply the first resurrection ever, as a matter of fact; its importance is not that there could be an entry in the *Guinness Book of Records*, 'Rising from the Dead: First Recorded Occurrence'. Jesus' resurrection is the first *in principle*.

But in saying all this I assumed that everyone present would take it for granted that Jesus was indeed the first person to rise to life from the dead: this I was treating as a given. After the service someone who knew his Bible very thoroughly said, 'I saw what you meant about the resurrection – that Jesus didn't just happen to be the first person to come back to life, that it isn't only that he was the first. But surely according to the Bible he wasn't *even* the first?' And he then listed all the other people in Scripture who rose from the dead: the children raised to life by Elijah (1 Kings 17.17–24) and Elisha (2 Kings 4.32–7), the widow's son at Nain (Luke 7.11–17), and Lazarus (John 11.38–44), not to mention the 'many bodies of the saints who had fallen asleep' who 'were raised, and coming out of the tombs after his resurrection . . . went into the holy city and appeared to many' (Matt. 27.52–3). Then he added, 'Anyway, there's plenty of evidence for survival after death from many religious traditions. So although I can see there's something special about Jesus himself, and specially his teaching, there's no sense in saying that his *resurrection* is unique.'

Taken off guard, I did not know how to reply to this; but I have since come to the conclusion that I was right in essence, though I expressed myself carelessly. The objection gave me much the same feeling as the Christians working for the local radio station had when they found their faith being equated with spooks and hauntings; for most of these stories of 'resurrections' do have, for me, a decidedly spooky flavour, even though they are in the Bible. They serve as evidence of the power and supremacy of God even over human death only so long as you don't think about them too closely. But when you begin to speculate on the implications, they become mysterious in the way the occult is mysterious, and they leave unanswered questions. What happened when the widow's son came to die again? What happened to those 'bodies of the saints' after they had appeared in Jerusalem? And Lazarus – what kind of a story did he tell his friends, when they had unwound him from his grave-clothes? No one has raised this last uncomfortable question more tellingly than Tennyson, in a passage which leaves me squeamishly feeling, How I wish you hadn't asked that:

> When Lazarus left his charnel-cave,
>   And home to Mary's house return'd,
>   Was this demanded – if he yearn'd
> To hear her weeping by his grave?
>
> 'Where wert thou, brother, those four days?'
>   There lives no record of reply,
>   Which telling what it is to die
> Had surely added praise to praise.
>
> From every house the neighbours met,
>   The streets were fill'd with joyful sound,
>   A solemn gladness even crown'd
> The purple brows of Olivet.
>
> Behold a man raised up by Christ!
>   The rest remaineth unreveal'd;
>   He told it not, or something seal'd
> The lips of that Evangelist.[1]

As well it might: this surely is not the world of what Christians mean by religion, so much as the world of the mystery story. Such speculations are fascinating, but the level at which they engage us has nothing much to do with *religion* as Christians understand the word, and says nothing about faith and trust in God as one we can know.

From time to time, the biblical record seems to suggest, there may arise those who can even bring the dead back into the world of the living – for a limited time. We may then be able to deduce a little about what death is, and what state the dead might be in; though the biblical writers (as Tennyson correctly saw) show little interest in the matter. But in any case these people die again. Nothing crucial or decisive turns on the event, however amazing and bewildering it may be. It is, we might say, simply a particularly spectacular example of healing the sick, analogous to a heart-transplant in the modern world. As modern people we may find such stories harder to believe than some of our forebears – though no one can ever have found them easy to believe, or why are they recorded with so much emphasis on their miraculous character? But they are essentially a matter of detail. Our overall perception of the world need not be altered, whether we believe in them or not. Nowhere is this clearer than in the extraordinary throw-away line in Matthew 10.5–8:

> These twelve Jesus sent out, charging them, 'Go nowhere among the Gentiles, and enter no town of the Samaritans, but go rather to the lost sheep of the house of Israel. And preach as you go, saying, "The kingdom of heaven is at hand." Heal the sick, *raise the dead*, cleanse lepers, cast out demons. You received without pay, give without pay.'

Raising the dead – to temporary new life – is merely one, not necessarily even the greatest, of the works the disciples are to perform in Jesus' name. It does not change the world.

The resurrection of Jesus is another matter. The evangelists are very sensitive to the suggestion that the risen Jesus is a ghost: they emphasize that he ate and drank, could be touched, and so on. But nor is he a resuscitated corpse. The atmosphere that emanates from the empty tomb is not the mysterious brooding sense of death temporarily cheated that wafts from Lazarus' 'charnel-cave'. It is a fresh, spring-like sense of totally new beginnings.

Last night did Christ the Sun rise from the dark,
  The mystic harvest of the fields of God,
And now the little wandering tribes of bees
  Are brawling in the scarlet flowers abroad.
The winds are soft with birdsong; all night long
  Darkling the nightingale her descant told,
And now inside church doors the happy folk
  The Alleluia chant a hundredfold.
O father of thy folk, be thine by right
The Easter joy, the threshold of the light.[2]

The man Mary Magdalene encountered walking freely in the garden with all the time in the world, so ordinary that she took him for the gardener, is poles apart from the revived Lazarus – still bound hand and foot and with his face covered, about to begin a new *lease* of life; until that lease falls in. In the Catholic and Orthodox churches the story of Lazarus is read, not in Eastertide, but at the end of Lent; it belongs to a time before Christ's resurrection, and is everything that true resurrection is not.

The difference between the resurrection of Christ and any anticipations of it there may have been, hung, as the first Christians saw it, on one decisive thing. The difference between Christian faith in the risen Christ, and all mere interest in the fringes and borders of religion, in ghosts and hauntings and things that go bump in the night, is put simply and unequivocally by St Paul. 'Christ being raised from the dead will never die again; death no longer has dominion over him' (Rom. 6.9). This sounds by now a platitude; but in the beginning it was the very heart of the gospel. In a culture where it was quite thinkable (though of course far from expected) that God might bring someone back to life by artificially reviving their corpse, there was something utterly distinctive about the idea of a resurrection that would never be followed by a second death. It was very quickly seen that this must imply that Jesus now existed in a quite fresh sphere of being, in a different 'place'; and there is good reason to think that many of the first Christians simply equated what we call the resurrection with what we call the ascension. For St Paul, Christ's being 'risen' means both that he has risen from the dead and that he has risen to sit at the right hand of God – he has, as it were, ascended from the grave into heaven. 'If then you have been raised with Christ, seek the things that are above, where Christ is, seated at the right hand of God' (Col. 3.1). To put it less spatially: Jesus' life was brought to an end by human malice, but that life is now lived out eternally in the presence of God. Death spells separation from God, for 'the dead do not praise the LORD, nor do any that go down into silence' (Ps. 115.17); in descending into the grave Jesus has been where God is not. But God will not have it so, since Jesus' life is a life he affirms and will not see extinguished; and therefore he reverses the separation of death, and ensures that Jesus is now and always wherever he is himself.

The Christian hope is that just because the essence of Jesus' life was his total availability to his followers and potentially to all mankind, we too can be associated with him in this new and divinely guaranteed life. We can be wherever Jesus is; and Jesus is at the heart of God himself. The experience of being 'risen with Christ' can begin now. It has nothing to do with physical death, and there is nothing in the least spooky about it. For Christians who can think in this way, their own survival of death, their own resurrection to eternal life with God, are assured, yet the details are not specially interesting: they are simply the obvious corollary of the relationship they have already entered into with the one who raised Jesus from the dead and made him sit at his right hand. Jesus' resurrection does not prove that there is life after death, still less that we should be interested in the paranormal; it proves whose side God is on, and holds out the assurance that he is not casual about his relationships. He does not add a bit on to good lives as a bonus. Rather, he associates those lives with the life of Jesus, who is united with him for ever. Life after death appears in this context almost as a by-product. It is not possible to say what resurrection life will be like, and to speculate greatly on it is out of place. 'Someone will ask, "How are the dead raised? With what kind of body do they come?" You foolish man!' (1 Cor. 15.35). The matter that is worth reflecting on is the character and love of the God who raised Jesus from the dead, and the promise of never being separated from him.

> Death be not proud, though some have called thee
> Mighty and dreadfull, for, thou art not soe,
> For, those, whom thou think'st, thou dost overthrow,
> Die not, poor death, nor yet canst thou kill me.
> From rest and sleepe, which but thy pictures bee,

Much pleasure, then from thee, much more must flow,
And soonest our best men with thee doe goe,
Rest of their bones, and soules deliverie.
Thou art slave to Fate, Chance, kings, and desperate men,
And dost with poyson, warre, and sicknesse dwell,
And poppie, or charmes can make us sleepe as well,
And better than thy stroke; why swell'st thou then?
One short sleepe past, wee wake eternally,
And death shall be no more; death, thou shalt die.[3]

Glory to the Father, who has woven garments of glory for the resurrection; worship to the Son, who was clothed in them at his rising; thanksgiving to the Spirit, who keeps them for all the saints; one nature in three, to him be praise.[4]

CHAPTER ELEVEN

Happy Endings

Entering the tomb, they saw a young man sitting on the right side, dressed in a white robe; and they were amazed. And he said to them, 'Do not be amazed; you seek Jesus of Nazareth, who was crucified. He has risen, he is not here; see the place where they laid him. But go, tell his disciples and Peter that he is going before you to Galilee; there you will see him, as he told you.' And they went out and fled from the tomb; for trembling and astonishment had come upon them; and they said nothing to any one, for they were afraid.

Mark 16.5–8

In the eighteenth century it was widely believed that good plays should have a 'happy ending'. *King Lear* was rewritten so as to end with Lear restored to the throne and Edgar married to Cordelia;[1] and Handel, making an oratorio of the terrible story of Jephthah's daughter (Judges 11.29–40) who is sacrificed by her father because he has vowed to offer to God the first person he meets on returning home from a successful military campaign, introduced a divine intervention (like the one which prevented the sacrifice of Isaac in Genesis 22) so that the girl's life should be spared after all. Taste in these matters changes, and most modern people feel that alterations like these simply ruin powerful tragedies.

Within the Bible itself, there are examples of happy endings that strike most people today as incongruous in much the same way. The Book of Job is the classic case. After Job has lost everything – possessions, health, and children – a lengthy dialogue between him and his 'comforters' plumbs the ultimate depths of human suffering and misery (Job 3—37); then God silences Job's protests and reduces him to abject submission. Readers used to modern literature with its willingness to confront ultimate despair feel, as seldom happens in reading the Bible, that they are getting their familiar food. But then the author spoils it all with a happy ending which seems banal beyond words. Job is restored to more than his original prosperity, with exactly twice as many flocks and herds, and ten more children to replace those he had lost. Our reaction to all this is likely to be that it ruins the entire story. Such acute

63

suffering is not to be wished away by magic, and the absurdity of thinking that seven new sons and three new daughters somehow compensate for the deaths of the original ones shows clearly that the story is being reduced to a childish level, with Job turning before our eyes from a profound tragic hero into a cardboard cut-out of the 'righteous man'. It is not surprising that many biblical scholars think the 'happy ending' of Job was added to the book by someone who shared much the same outlook that came to prevail in the eighteenth century; the original author, perhaps, had an understanding which is nearer to our own of what makes a good plot.

We react adversely to these 'improvements' to tragic stories because we feel that happy endings like these are not really *endings* at all, but mere appendages. We are not prepared to think of the great characters who suffer in the pages of Shakespeare or the Bible as though they lived in a world governed by different principles from the real world; and we know that in the real world suffering is not a matter of unhappy external events which can be cancelled out by happy ones, provided these are 'greater' according to some yardstick by which the magnitude of suffering or joy is to be measured. A satisfying plot for us must respect the depths of the characters who act it out, and if they are as profound as Job it will not do to reward them with mere external bonuses to compensate for their losses. We feel cheated, as the facile happy ending makes a mockery of our previous feeling that we were reading something profound and haunting.

By contrast, a really satisfying ending can challenge the understanding we thought we had of the story in ways that deepen that understanding rather than undermine it. A 'proper' ending to a novel or play resolves the ambiguity of the plot and shows us where the story had been going all along – whether for good or ill. It is in the literal sense a *dénouement*, an 'unknotting' of the uncertainties and confusions of the plot. In its light we see what this or that mysterious character was doing in the story, why the hero spoke as he did, who the stranger in the second act really was, and so on. In a good detective novel, all the pieces suddenly fall into place in the light of the ending. But detective novels are only the extreme case of something that is true of all well-constructed plots, whether comic or tragic: the ending 'makes sense of' all that has gone before; it is not an optional addition to the story, but its resolution.

Now it is very attractive for Christians to see the great events of

Jesus' life, death, and resurrection as a supreme drama, and to interpret them with some of the insights that come from our experience of drama in the literal sense of the word. We shall rightly want to resist seeing the resurrection of Jesus as a facile 'happy ending', as though God waved a magic wand and replaced the horrific suffering of the cross with a brand-new life in which all pain was simply wiped away. As we have already seen, it was important to the evangelists to stress that Christ's wounds remained in his risen body; even though it was so transformed that he was at first unrecognizable, still it was the same Jesus, and the wounds remained:

> By these same scars his men
> Beheld the very body that they knew,
> No transient breath,
> No drift of bodiless air,
> And held him in their hearts in fortress there.[2]

The risen Christ is not a *replacement* for the crucified Jesus, as Job's fresh sons and daughters were a replacement for those he had lost; the risen Christ *is* the crucified Jesus, the same person in a new (and endless) life. And a good way of putting this may seem to lie through the idea of death and resurrection as a single drama. Let me develop this a little, but then point out its limitations.

The resurrection of Jesus, as we have already seen, is not a 'mere' past event, a single nugget of interesting information to be placed alongside other unusual and striking historical events: 'snow once fell in London in June'; 'the birth of octuplets has occasionally occurred'; 'Jesus Christ rose from the dead in the first century AD'. The resurrection of Jesus is good news, and it is good news because it is an event which carries a heavy weight of meaning. Thomas's reaction when he recognizes the risen Lord is not 'So the dead can rise, after all; how fascinating', but 'My Lord and my God!' In acknowledging that Jesus is risen we are not merely accepting that a surprising historical event did, after all, occur. We are saying that the puzzling and ambiguous story of Jesus that the Gospels tell has in its entirety to be understood in one way rather than another. The fact that the person of whom the story tells rose from the dead, never to die again, makes it a different kind of story. The resurrection is the *dénouement* of the story of Jesus, and like all such endings it has a retroactive effect on the whole 'plot' of the Gospel account. It is God's assertion that Jesus was not a good idea which went disastrously wrong, not an unfortunate footnote in the random historical process, but the core and centre of his whole plan for humanity. This life was supremely the kind of life that could be made eternal, the only life which could be reaffirmed without qualification as the meeting-point of time and eternity.

Thus the resurrection is the ultimate example of a true 'happy ending', one which is perfectly congruous with the story it concludes. Suddenly it all makes sense. For the resurrection confers on us the gift of hindsight, and we can see, in a flash, that all these things happened not (as we might have thought) as part of the endless contingencies of human life, but as stages in a great divine plan.

> Then he opened their minds to understand the scriptures, and said to them, 'Thus it is written, that the Christ should suffer and on the third day rise from the dead' (Luke 24.45-6).

Jesus' life, death, and resurrection can thus be seen as a drama in three acts, of which God himself is the author. And the drama is, in the technical sense, a comedy rather than a tragedy; not in the superficial sense that a happy ending has been stuck on to a play that was designed to be tragic, but in the profound sense that the suffering (which is real) ends in such supreme joy that 'death is swallowed up in victory'. Indeed, the light of the resurrection shines back even beyond the birth of Jesus, to 'the dark backward and abysm of time'. As the old legend of the 'harrowing of hell' reminds us, Christ's resurrection rescues not just himself, the crucified Jesus, and not just those who would subsequently come to believe in him, but those too who lived before his coming, 'the spirits in prison' (1 Pet. 3.19). He rescued them, and with them all past history, showing it to be not (in Eliot's words) 'waste sad time',[3] but an outpost of eternity. Even the sins and errors that seem, from our perspective, to distort it thus have their place in God's greater scheme: 'O truly necessary sin of Adam, which by the death of Christ was done away; O happy fault, which was counted worthy to have such and so great a Redeemer!' says the Church's Easter proclamation, the ancient text known as the *Exultet*.

Literary critics in ancient and modern times (the eighteenth century is a rare exception) have generally judged that tragedy is a more profound genre than comedy; but in Christianity tragedy is revealed as the lesser of the two. Notoriously, Christians have for that very reason found it hard to write good tragedies; optimism insists on breaking through. For the story of Christ in the Gospels is not a tragedy artificially transmuted into a banal comedy, like Tate's *Lear*. Properly understood, it is a comedy through and through, though on so high a level and with so much human pain enfolded within it that we almost miss the joy, and only the eye of faith will enable us to cry out with Thomas, 'My Lord and my God!' Only Jesus himself, perhaps, saw the end from the beginning, and 'for the joy that was set before him endured the cross, despising the shame, and is seated at the right hand of the throne of God' (Heb. 12.2).

The gospel as a great comedy which has come true: a powerful idea. And yet: to call the gospel message a story or a drama is I believe ultimately to domesticate it, and to try to contain it within categories of human devising. Comedy and tragedy alike are systems within which we try to encapsulate human experience, but the experience itself outstrips them both. We reject bad comedy and bad tragedy as 'untrue to life', but the truth is that good drama is also 'untrue'; we are not really characters in a plot, not even a well-constructed one. To see Jesus' life and work as a tragedy is, indeed, to ignore the resurrection, and to think of him as a great but doomed hero. But to think of it as a comedy, thus allowing the resurrection so much to illuminate the suffering that went before it that the cross itself becomes a place of light, is also flawed. St John's Gospel goes down this road, presenting the moment of Jesus' death as the moment of glory, and Christian tradition has often followed the same path: 'Since it brings life, the tomb of Christ is lovelier indeed than paradise; it is the fountain whence our resurrection springs', says an Eastern Orthodox text. But whatever truth there is in this tradition, it is very hard for it to avoid losing a sharp sense of the arbitrariness, the cruel and casual character of the Lord's suffering and death; and in the process also the sense of uncovenanted and unlooked-for joy in the resurrection. Happy endings stuck artificially on to tales of woe will not satisfy us, and one can see at once that the resurrection is not in that category. But a happy ending which has the effect of rewriting what precedes it, turning the whole account into a smooth and beautifully executed masterpiece of planned comedy – this, too, fails to ring true as an account of the effect the Gospels have on us.

Somehow there needs to be a third possibility. For though the resurrection narratives are indeed written with some literary skill, yet their effect is in a mysterious way more than literary. The resurrection is a shock; and not a contrived shock, a kind of dramatic finesse, but a real shock – the shock when we hear of a sudden and accidental death, or the shock of love at first sight. Such experiences are opposite in value, but very similar in quality; and neither produces the smile of the well-satisfied drama critic, but the pounding heart and physical disorientation of the person whom reality has suddenly struck down. 'They went out and fled from the tomb; for trembling and astonishment had come upon them; and they said nothing to any one, for they were afraid.'

Between crucifixion and resurrection there is an unbridgeable gap. Certainly, it is not the gap that exists between a good tragedy and an artificially added happy ending. But nor is it the kind of gap that invites us to reread the story in order to integrate it into some higher unity – like a tell-tale inconsistency in a detective story, pointing to the solution of the mystery. The space between death and resurrection – Jesus' and ours – is a real space, the space in which darkness reigned and might have gone on reigning for ever. The light that breaks from the tomb on Easter morning is like the light of the first day of creation: utterly new, wholly unexpected, completely unforeseeable. It is not part of a carefully honed divine plan which could in principle have been known. The crucifixion and the resurrection are not successive acts in the same drama; they belong essentially to two quite different stories, the story of what human malice can perpetrate and the story of what God's love can accomplish. They defeat all our attempts to incorporate them into one single, overarching scheme. And the joy of the resurrection is not the sense of relief and pleasure that, after all, the story turned out well in the end; it is (as J.R.R. Tolkien put it), a 'joy beyond the walls of the world, poignant as grief'.[4]

O Eternal Wisdom,
we praise you and give you thanks,
because the beauty of death could not contain you.
You broke forth from the comfort of the grave;
before you the stone was moved,
and the tomb of our world was opened wide.

For on this day you were raised in power
and revealed yourself to the women
as a beloved stranger,
offering for the rituals of the dead
the terror of new life
and of desire fulfilled.[5]

CHAPTER TWELVE

Unveiled Faces

Now the Lord is the Spirit, and where the Spirit of the Lord is, there is freedom. And we all, with unveiled faces, beholding the glory of the Lord, are being changed into his likeness from one degree of glory to another; for this comes from the Lord who is the Spirit. Therefore, having this ministry by the mercy of God, we do not lose heart. We have renounced disgraceful, under-handed ways; we refuse to practise cunning or to tamper with God's word, but by the open statement of the truth we would commend ourselves to every man's conscience in the sight of God. And even if our gospel is veiled, it is veiled only to those who are perishing. In their case the god of this world has blinded the minds of the unbelievers, to keep them from seeing the light of the gospel of the glory of Christ, who is the likeness of God. For what we preach is not ourselves, but Jesus Christ as Lord, with ourselves as your servants for Jesus' sake. For it is the God who said, 'Let light shine out of darkness,' who has shone in our hearts to give the light of the knowledge of the glory of God in the face of Christ.

2 Corinthians 3.17—4.6

Sometimes on a journey your train passes another, and unexpectedly slows down; and you suddenly see someone in the carriage that is passing yours who seems to be looking you straight in the face. In reality they are just staring out of the window, and are not expecting their eyes to meet yours any more than you are expecting to meet theirs. You have no other contact with them, and only a split second to take them in. Sometimes you find yourself staring into a face that is tranquil and at peace. But sometimes it is vacant in a hopeless way, and sometimes it is full of anger or fear. Just for that moment you are looking into someone's face without their having had a chance to prepare for the encounter – without time to put on their emotional make-up; and you have not had that chance either. In that moment you see them without their defences, and you get an inkling of what they are when there is no one there; what they are, we might say, in the presence of God.

The person whose unguarded face is open and welcoming is

a most attractive sight, but such people are not so common as one might hope. When what I see in such an unprepared face is aggression or fear or despair, I begin to wonder what the people I think I know look like when they, too, are off their guard; and then, what I look like myself. For what we know of others, even of those we think we know well, is that part of themselves that they turn towards us; and beyond that there is the vast area which is like the far side of the moon, never available for our inspection. When we hear that someone has done something very uncharacteristic – a criminal act, a piece of untypical malice, something self-destructive – we suddenly realize that we did not know them as we thought we did; but then we should reflect how little we really know anyone. When I am alone, no one is there to see what I do, how I behave, or how I look; yet what I am when I am alone is a very large part of me, perhaps the largest part. And no one knows what it is like; for no one is there.

Christians believe that the God who raised Jesus from the dead invites them to look into his face, and to meet his gaze, and that he is as prepared for this encounter as he wishes them to be. There are two ways in which Christians believe that they can gaze, so to speak, into the eyes of God. The first is through Jesus – which means in practice through learning about Jesus from the pages of the New Testament and from the tradition of teaching about him that the Church has received, and through prayer and personal reflection on that teaching. A Christian is, by definition, someone who believes that God shows himself to us through Jesus: that Jesus is the face God presents to the world. It is through this life, this death, this resurrection that God makes himself known; Jesus' values are the values God tells us are his own, Jesus' life is the kind of life God tells us he is committed to. This is the human face of God; when we are in God's presence, he chooses to look out on us through Jesus' eyes, and to tell us that this is the definitive picture of himself we are to believe in.

The second way we get to know God is through all the traces of his presence that sensitivity to him enables us to find in the world about us, in nature, in the lives of others, in our own experience. This is what is meant by the activity of the Holy Spirit: all the ways in which God impinges on our lives by shaping them, making them flourish, drawing out what potential they have for good. We do not 'see' the Holy Spirit, but we experience his activity as the power by which we see everything else more clearly, and are enabled to find God in every part of our life. The Spirit, in fact, is the way God chooses that we shall feel him at work in ourselves; and Christians believe that wherever people flourish and blossom, there God is at work through the Spirit. God wants us to think of himself as present in such positive and creative experiences.

Thus the work of the Spirit and the character of Jesus are two aspects of the face of God, as it is turned towards his world. When our eyes meet his, and both of us are prepared for the encounter, this is what we see.

No doubt Christians who are aware of their own failings will recognize many occasions when they were *not* prepared, and so did not see what they should have seen. But some may have allowed a much more terrible thought to surface in their minds. God, of course, is always prepared for the encounter with us, and so he is never off his guard. But what should we see if he were? What if God is really like the person on the train? Suppose that the character of Jesus, and the work of the Holy Spirit, are what God wants us to believe about himself – the work, you might say, of his public relations department – but that beyond them lies the wholly unknown nature of God as he is in himself: a great sea of mystery in which we do not really know him at all. Even with another human being, as we have seen, the face that is turned towards us is far less than the whole person. With God, what we feel we know can surely be no more than the tiniest fragment, a speck of sand among all the sand on thousands of millions of stars. What if the true nature of God, God as he is when no one is looking, is really quite different from the person revealed in Jesus and known through the Holy Spirit?

An abyss of doubt and horror here opens at our feet. Yet mystics and theologians down the ages have been haunted by this idea, and have warned that God is indeed ultimately vast, mysterious, unknowable, and hidden from our gaze. 'Be not rash with your mouth, nor let your heart be hasty to utter a word before God, for God is in heaven, and you upon earth; therefore let your words be few' (Eccles. 5.2). And so even as we rejoice that in the resurrection of Jesus and in the gift of the Spirit God has given us some inkling of his nature, we should not be so presumptuous as to think that it is ultimate truth. It is what God wants us to believe; and in all humility, it may be felt, that should be enough for us. Who are we to claim more?

But I believe that this particular exercise in spiritual and intellectual modesty owes more to suspicion than to humility, and that the Christian gospel can hardly survive at all if it is qualified like this. Jesus' resurrection is not the final act of a play God has written to give us a good but potentially misleading impression of what he is like. Jesus' resurrection is the act of God as he really is, the consistent and wholehearted God who cannot lie and does not deceive us. Yes, God is greater than anything we can know fully; but no, God is not an enigma, he is not the dark side of the moon. When we know what God chooses to reveal about himself, through Christ and through the Spirit, it is his true self that he reveals; and in God there is no inconsistency, there is no putting on a face, no falsity or pretence. Jesus is not the face God likes to show the world; Jesus is what God is really like. The work of the Holy Spirit in our lives is not the work of God's propaganda department; it is the work of God himself.

> O Father, give the spirit power to climb
> To the fountain of all light, and be purified.
> Break through the mists of earth,
>   the weight of the clod,
> Shine forth in splendour, Thou that art calm weather,
> And quiet resting place for faithful souls.
> To see thee is the end and the beginning,
> Thou carriest us, and thou dost go before,
> Thou art the journey, and the journey's end.[1]

These are among the truths that the doctrine of the Trinity is designed to safeguard: that the God we know in Christ and in the Spirit is the living and true God, and that there is no God beyond him, and no realms within his infinite being where he is unlike what we know of him by those routes. Sometimes in the Church today this doctrine of the Trinity is presented as a way of emphasizing how mysterious God is. But whatever truth there may be in saying that God is mysterious, the doctrine of the Trinity is the very last doctrine that expresses it. For what it declares is that the God who is beyond all our conceptions and our power to imagine him *has made himself known* in Jesus and continues to reveal himself through the work of the Spirit in the world; and in these ways that he reveals himself, it is genuinely himself that he reveals, not something less than his true self, not what he wants us to believe, not what we can stand, but the truth.

The Christian hope is that, when at last we come to see God as he is and to know him as he knows us, we shall recognize him; for we shall see in him 'with unveiled faces' all that we have known in Jesus and through the work of the Holy Spirit. *God the known* is the theme of the Christian gospel. In it we have the assurance that the heart that beats in heaven is a heart of love, the same heart that led Jesus to his death because he loved his fellow men and women, the same heart that beats in all those who have experienced the work of the Spirit to transform their lives and make them flourish.

In his poem 'Wrestling Jacob' Charles Wesley reflected on the strange story in Genesis 32.22–32 where Jacob wrestles all night with an angel (or, perhaps, with God) to discover his name: that is, his nature. In the story God refuses to reveal it, though he blesses Jacob; but in Christ, says Wesley, God's true nature *is* at last revealed; and it is love.

> Come, O Thou Traveller unknown,
>   Whom still I hold, but cannot see,
> My company before is gone,
>   And I am left alone with Thee;
> With Thee all night I mean to stay,
> And wrestle till the break of day.
>
> I need not tell Thee who I am,
>   My misery or sin declare;
> Thyself hast call'd me by my name;
>   Look on Thy hands, and read it there!
> But Who, I ask Thee, Who art Thou?
> Tell me Thy name, and tell me now.
>
> Wilt Thou not yet to me reveal
>   Thy new, unutterable Name?
> Tell me, I still beseech Thee, tell:
>   To know it now, resolved I am:
> Wrestling, I will not let Thee go,
> Till I Thy Name, Thy Nature know.

Yield to me now, for I am weak,
  But confident in self-despair;
Speak to my heart, in blessings speak,
  Be conquer'd by my instant prayer!
Speak, or Thou never hence shalt move, –
And tell me, if Thy Name is Love?

– 'Tis Love! 'tis Love! Thou diedst for me!
  I hear Thy whisper in my heart!
The morning breaks, the shadows flee;
  Pure universal Love Thou art!
To me, to all, Thy bowels move;
Thy Nature and Thy Name is Love!

My prayer hath power with GOD; the grace
  Unspeakable I now receive;
Through faith I see Thee face to face,
  I see Thee face to face, and live:
In vain I have not wept and strove;
Thy Nature and Thy Name is Love.

I know Thee, Saviour, Who Thou art;
  JESUS, the feeble sinner's Friend!
Nor wilt Thou with the night depart,
  But stay, and love me to the end!
Thy mercies never shall remove –
Thy Nature and Thy Name is Love!

We rejoice with all the saints
that when Christ who is our life appears
we also shall appear with him in glory:
and we pray that in the freedom of the Spirit
we all, with unveiled face,
reflecting the glory of the Lord
may be changed into his likeness
from glory to glory.[2]

Notes

FOREWORD

1 Janet Morley, *All Desires Known* (London, Movement for the Ordination of Women, 1988).

2 John Austin Baker, *The Foolishness of God* (London, Darton, Longman and Todd, 1970).

CHAPTER 1 The Necessary Path

1 From the hymn 'O sacred head, sore wounded' – Robert Bridges' translation of '*O Haupt voll Blut und Wunden*' by Paul Gerhardt (1607–76), which was in turn based on the fourteenth-century Latin hymn '*Salve caput cruentatum*', ascribed to St Bernard of Clairvaux. The German original does not, however, imply participation in Christ's sufferings in the same way as Bridges' translation; Gerhardt as a good Lutheran would have been deeply suspicious of Christians who sought to identify their own sufferings with those of Jesus.

2 William Blake, 'Auguries of Innocence', *c.* 1803.

3 William Blake, 'The Divine Image', from *Songs of Innocence*, 1789.

4 *All Desires Known*, p. 14.

CHAPTER 2 The Outsider

1 For what follows I am indebted to Gerd Theissen, *Biblical Faith: an Evolutionary Approach*, London, SCM Press, 1985, and *The Shadow of the Galilean*, London, SCM Press, 1987.

2 Paulinus of Nola (353–431), '*Verbum crucis*', tr. in Helen Waddell, *Medieval Latin Lyrics* (London, Constable, 1929; Penguin Books, 1952), pp. 50–1.

3 From 'Lord, it belongs not to my care' by Richard Baxter (1615–91).

4 *All Desires Known*, p. 8.

CHAPTER 3 Time and Chance

1 David Brown, 'The Problem of Pain', in Robert Morgan, ed., *The Religion of the Incarnation: Anglican Essays in Commemoration of* Lux Mundi (Bristol, Bristol Classical Press, 1989), pp. 46–59; the quotation is assembled from several paragraphs on pp. 54–7.

2 Thomas Aquinas (*c.*1225–74), '*Verbum supernum prodiens*', tr. in Helen Waddell, *More Latin Lyrics from Virgil to Milton: Edited and with an Introduction by Dame Felicitas Corrigan* (London, Victor Gollancz, 1980), pp. 304–5.

3 *All Desires Known*, p. 15.

CHAPTER 4 God's Cross

1 Ignatius, *Romans* 7; tr. Maxwell Staniforth, rev. Andrew Louth in *Early Christian Writings: The Apostolic Fathers* (London, Penguin Books, 1987), p. 87.

2 In an article in *The Sunday Times*; but I have failed to trace it.

3 Helen Waddell, *Peter Abelard* (London, Constable, 1933), pp. 268–70. There is a sympathetic presentation of (the real) Abelard's much misunderstood theory of the atonement in Paul S. Fiddes, *Past Event and Present Salvation: The Christian Idea of Atonement*, London, Darton, Longman and Todd, 1989.

4 Raymond Hockley, *Intercessions at Holy Communion on Themes for the Church's Year* (London and Oxford, Mowbray, 1981), p. 20.

CHAPTER 5 Christ Crucified

1 Alfred Tennyson, *In Memoriam*, 1850, Prologue.
2 From 'My God! my God! and can it be?' by F.W. Faber (1814–63).
3 George Herbert, 'The Call', in *The Temple*, 1633.
4 *All Desires Known*, p. 23.

CHAPTER 6 Perfect Freedom

1 For the ideas in this paragraph, compare W.H. Vanstone, *The Stature of Waiting*, London, Darton, Longman and Todd, 1982.
2 Boethius (480–*c*.524), *de consolatione philosophiae* 1.4, tr. in *More Latin Lyrics*, pp. 94–5.
3 The phrase is taken from Helen Waddell, *Peter Abelard*, p. 282.
4 George Herbert, 'The Agonie', in *The Temple*.
5 *All Desires Known*, p. 21.

CHAPTER 7 Down into Silence

1 Peter Abelard (1079–1142), Hymn for the Third Nocturn at Matins on Good Friday; tr. in *Medieval Latin Lyrics*, pp. 178–9.
2 *All Desires Known*, p. 16.

CHAPTER 8 The Stranger

1 There are very illuminating comments on this in Rowan Williams, *Resurrection: Interpreting the Easter Gospel*, London, Darton, Longman and Todd, 1982, especially in chapter 2, 'Memory and Hope: Easter in Galilee'. See p. 29: 'God is the agency that gives us back our memories, because God is the "presence" to which all reality is present.'
2 Theodulf of Orleans (*c*.750–821), 'Wherefore the scars of Christ's passion remained in the body of his resurrection', tr. in *More Latin Lyrics*, pp. 210–13. One stanza has been omitted, but it appears on p. 65 below.
3 *All Desires Known*, p. 16.

CHAPTER 9 Christian Names

1 On this see again Rowan Williams, *Resurrection*, especially pp. 29–43.
2 *The Rubáiyát of Omar Khayyám*, tr. Edward Fitzgerald (London 1859), no. 51. Whether this – one of the most famous of all Fitzgerald's stanzas – represents anything like what Omar Khayyám wrote I am in no position to say.
3 *All Desires Known*, p. 26.

CHAPTER 10 The Death of Death

1 *In Memoriam*, § 31.
2 Sedulius Scottus (*fl.*848–74), '*Carmen Paschale*', tr. in *Medieval Latin Lyrics*, pp. 130–1.
3 John Donne, *Holy Sonnets* 10, 1633.
4 A Syrian Orthodox prayer: see George Appleton, ed., *The Oxford Book of Prayer* (Oxford, Oxford University Press, 1985), p. 255.

CHAPTER 11 Happy Endings

1 The adaptation was made by Nahum Tate in 1681 and was the standard acting version until 1843. The text can be found in Montague Summers, *Shakespeare Adaptations*, London 1922.

2 Theodulf of Orleans, 'Wherefore the scars of Christ's passion remained in the body of his resurrection'; see note 2 to chapter 8, above. This is the remaining stanza.

3 T.S. Eliot, 'Burnt Norton' 5, *Four Quartets*, London, Faber and Faber 1944.

4 J.R.R. Tolkien, 'On Fairy-stories', in *Essays Presented to Charles Williams*, London, Oxford University Press, 1947; reprinted with minor revisions in *Tree and Leaf* (London, Unwin, 1964), pp. 11–70. The quotation is from p. 60.

5 *All Desires Known*, p. 42.

CHAPTER 12 Unveiled Faces

1 Boethius, *de consolatione philosophiae* 3.9, lines 22–8; tr. in *More Latin Lyrics*, pp. 112–13.

2 *Intercessions at Holy Communion*, p. 31.

Also by John Barton and published by SPCK

PEOPLE OF THE BOOK?

The Authority of the Bible in Christianity

'John Barton's Bampton Lectures for 1988, so speedily brought to print, delighted and edified those who heard them. Their subject could not be more topical or the treatment more compelling. This is a book for those who feel uncertain and discouraged in face of the confidence of fundamentalist tendencies: those who know in their bones that what they are told is crude and unsatisfactory but who are easily caught out in particular cases by the seemingly greater zeal or piety of the others. These lectures are written with every commendable degree of clarity, honesty and fidelity to both Christian truth and Christian life.'   *Theology*

'. . . one of the very best counter-arguments published in recent years to the insidious pervasive influence of contemporary fundamentalism . . . in a deceptively simple but very carefully argued work, John Barton brings a scholarly rigour to bear upon biblicism in a book marked as much by his love and respect for the text of scripture as by his knowledge of, and attention to, critical method.'   *Ministry*

'The purpose of a good book is surely to interest, to stimulate, to challenge and to provoke; and I have found that Dr Barton does all of these things on almost every page . . . no one should miss reading this book. It is a tract for our times.'   *Church Times*

**Available from all good bookshops, or in case of
difficulty contact SPCK Mail Order, 36 Steep Hill,
Lincoln LN2 1LU**